Old World Breads
and the

History of a Flemish Baker

Also by Charel Scheele:

Old World Breads
More Old Breads . . . & Soups Too
Adobe Oven for Old World Breads
Old World Breads from Your Bread Machine

Old World Breads
and the

History of a Flemish Baker

CHAREL SCHEELE

Old World Breads and the History of a Flemish Baker

iUniverse books may be ordered through booksellers or by contacting:

iUniverse
1663 Liberty Drive
Bloomington, IN 47403
www.iuniverse.com
844-349-9409

ISBN: 978-1-4620-5471-8 (sc)
ISBN: 978-1-4620-5472-5 (e)

Print information available on the last page.

iUniverse rev. date: 10/02/2020

Table of Contents

To Ingrid, whose encouragement and help were invaluable in the writing of this book.

Preface

As a professional baker, at one time and another on both continents, the European and the American, I would like to share with the readers some of my knowledge of bread baking and also some of the experiences I had in my life as a baker during the Second World War.

I grew up in a family of bakers, a trade which by European tradition is passed on from father to son for generations. After finishing school I attended a special 2 year-school for bread bakers. Then, I went for another 2 years to a specialized school for bakers and pastry chefs. I graduated from both schools with high honors.

During the times that I was not a professional baker, I baked bread as a hobby and many times I entered my products in local and State fairs, and I won blue ribbons for all the presentations.

At some of the classes and lectures I gave on the subject of bread making I have been asked about how life was during the dark period of the German occupation of The Netherlands. Now that I am at the seven score and ten of my life, I am surprised how the knowledge of that time has dwindled in the minds of many, to the point that some cannot or do not want to remember what happened in those historical years. Most of the survivors of that terrible time are old and a lot would rather forget the things they went thru then. I do feel people need to know what happened, so that history will not be repeated. So, in this book I am telling my story. Since I found out that bread making can be a very enjoyable process to work out negative emotions one experiences in troubled times. I have included some of my favorite bread recipes so that others can work out their frustrations in life by kneading and punching the dough, and enjoy the delectable results in wonderfully made loaves of bread.

Due to many requests, in this book I also have included the history of the spelt grain and recipes with sourdough free of commercial yeast and wheat, for people that have allergies to wheat and yeast.

With this book I hope to share some of the history of my life during the Second World War with accounts that include not only tragedy but also humorous anecdotes. Since baking was part of my life, I like to share my knowledge of bread making, with recipes and tips on healthy and delicious eating. Most importantly, I also want to share how the Bible can help in changing our outlook in life and give us hope for a better future.

A synopsis of my life

I was born in the late 1920's in a small village close to Gouda, South Holland, as the 16th child in a family of twenty. The family baking business was run at that time by my uncle, my father's younger brother. I am his namesake. Since he and his wife did not have children, at the age of twelve I was entrusted to them to be raised and educated with the purpose of eventually taking over the business, which consisted of a very successful flour mill and several bakeries in Axel, in the Dutch part of the Flanders.

During the time I was raised at my father's home, childhood was pleasant. I started school at the age of 6, having to walk a good three quarters of a mile to and fro. Since there was no cafeteria, we also had to walk to and fro during the noon hour to have our lunch at home. After school I had lots of siblings to play with, and also lots of neighborhood kids for games of street soccer. At home the atmosphere was usually intense as most conversations centered on political themes. In 1933 Hitler came to power in Germany. My mother was very much opposed to his ideas, and my father thought that he would be the salvation of Europe. That made for many interesting and sometimes heated disputes at the dinner table. They also read the Bible daily, like a ritual, with minimal or almost no religious instructions.

At my uncle's house, things were different. They were very religious in another denomination. So my father made the stipulation that I did not have to attend their church. Because of this my aunt thought I was godless and she told me I would burn in hell for it. Since I did not know the Bible, I believed her.

Now, after school I had no more time to play. After homework, I had to work hard sweeping the floor of the bakery, preparing the bread pans, and helping to carry in the firewood for the oven. They told me I had to learn the business from the ground up. So, as the years went by, I learned every aspect of the trade.

Since I was halfway convinced that I would go to hell, as a teenager, I decided to enjoy my life without restraints because I figured that's all I had. So on Sundays I started going to pool halls, enjoying a beer or two, and later more, to the point that, as a young adult I came home inebriated a lot of the times. Other bad habits followed, like smoking and gambling. When my parents came to visit, my aunt always told them what a good boy I was, and all my vices were covered over with good descriptions of my behavior.

Part of my job was to deliver freshly baked bread to regular customers on a bike route. One of my customers was an old lady who knew her Bible and she often would quote to me several passages. One time she told me that the Bible does not teach the idea of a burning hell. That was of interest to me as I knew that would be my ultimate destination. She then showed me Revelation 20:14 where the Bible explains the meaning of the lake of fire. I asked her where did she learned all those things and she told me about the meetings of Jehovah's Witnesses. So, out of curiosity I began to attend such meetings.

Because of these Christian meetings, it was not long before I started to change my behavior to conform to the truths that I was learning from the Bible. My family found out about my attending the meetings of Jehovah's Witnesses. This caused them to be very hostile toward me. In their religious prejudice and hatred of this group they told me I had a choice to make; either to be accepted at home and by the family and run the business or to follow the dictates of this despised sect. I told them I wanted to follow the dictates of my own conscience. I knew that some of the beliefs of my family were just traditions, and not Bible based, and so, I could no longer live by the dictates of their conscience. Since this caused a rift in the order of things acceptable by them they decided to disown and disinherit me and to sell their business to a stranger.

I migrated to Ontario, Canada where at that time four of my brothers lived. In order to earn a living and to learn English I got a job at a farm. On the first Sunday off I hitched a ride to the town of St. Thomas. Since I could not speak English, I had a hard time finding a Kingdom Hall, which is the place that the Jehovah's Witnesses meet. I could not make myself understood to a lot of passersby. Finally, an old man sitting on a bench with a Watchtower magazine on his lap, was able to direct me to the Hall, which was quite a distance away. There I found a couple from Belgium that spoke Flemish and they were able to further my education in the Bible.

In 1960 I migrated to the United States and from 1962 until 1967 I was able to work as a volunteer baker at the headquarters of Jehovah's Witnesses in Brooklyn, NY. There I received the best education I had in the Bible, and I would not have traded that for all the bakeries and flourmills in the world. Even now in my eighties, I am very happy that I made the right decision to follow the dictates of my own conscience.

Growing up during the Second World War

In May 1940, Hitler gave orders to invade the Netherlands, Belgium and Luxembourg. Life as we knew then changed drastically. Most food items were confiscated and shipped to Germany. In order to purchase food we had to have ration cards. People who were considered enemies of the regime, those of a different ethnic origin and the mentally ill could not get ration cards and had to survive by whatever means they could. Bakers could no longer purchase the wheat flour needed to run their business. At the beginning of the occupation most of them could only acquire half of their supply of flour. So a lot of experimentation took place. Some added potato, barley or any legume flour they could find. I remember that sometimes the bread was so hard and compact, that it was almost impossible to slice it with a knife. At least, we still had bread.

Since most manufactured goods were shipped to Germany, clothing, furniture and household items were simply not available. As the war went on, the situation became worse, and life became severely austere. Since there were spies and snitches everywhere, people could no longer express their opinions or show any discontent. The ones who did just disappeared overnight. Others, like Jews, Gypsies and Jehovah's Witnesses, were terribly mistreated. Fear and tension were palpable in the air.

Even under adversity children many times find a way to express playfulness. Now, besides soccer, we also had war games. We played with wooden guns. The kids in the next street were our enemies and vice-versa. Having observed how soldiers shaved the heads of the prisoners of war, we decided to do the same when one of the kids from another street walked in our territory. So we held poor Ulter Zwijndrecht prisoner and clipped his hair. His mother was so mad that she went to the police station to denounce us. However the police had more serious considerations to take care of, and so she decided to take matters on her own hands and she came after us with a broom stick. War can create a hostile environment even among neighbors who before were at peace with one another.

On another occasion, in June 1940, there was a large group of Germans soldiers resting on a grassy field not far from the street where we kids were playing. One of the soldiers motioned for us to come over. He then gave us some money and a canteen and told us to buy some good warm Dutch beer. Three of us ran to a tavern and got the canteen filled with dark beer. On the way back we wondered about the taste, and we all took some good gulps of it. Then we realized that the canteen was about twenty percent empty. One of the boys just knew that now we were going to be shot. I had to urinate and went behind a tree. The other boys handed me the canteen and told me to fill it up. So I did. Back at the grassy field we gave the German soldier his canteen. He grinned from ear to ear and told us to keep the change. Then he took a big swallow of it and immediately spit it out saying: "Yuck! Those stupid Dutch don't know how to brew good beer like the Germans do"! And before he could do anything, all the soldiers were called to attention and we didn't stay around. Later we replayed that scene many times and Ulter Zwijndrecht, the same boy who had gotten his hair shaved by us, could impersonate the German soldier so well, that we had many good laughs together, and so the previous incident was forgiven.

As the war continued on, life became tougher and tougher. Everything was rationed, or unavailable. Many were dying of starvation. In the winters things became even worse.

The winter of 1944 was especially brutal. In early December the German soldiers were spray painting all their vehicles white. We thought that they were getting ready for the snowy Russian frontline. The white color would be a good camouflage for the snow. However they were getting ready for the Ardennes offensive, which later became known as the Battle of the Bulge. Since Hitler had lowered the draft age, most of the soldiers were 16 and 17 years old. Thousands upon thousands on both sides of the War died in that battle, soldiers and civilians. Some villages were wiped out while other places suffered only a few casualties.

Hitler had ordered that every man 16 years old and upward from the occupied territory of the Netherlands be brought to Germany to work in the armament industry. The SS began to conduct what we called "razias". This was a raid to round up men at gunpoint, at night, under the cover of darkness, to catch the people off guard. They did this house to house, invading every home, looking for young men to send off to Germany. To avoid being picked up by the SS, my brother Joost and I often slept in an old abandoned utility trailer. From the small one foot window we could see the back of our house across the pond. Our mother would hang a bed sheet on the clothes line. That was the sign for us that it was safe to come home, as the razia was over. We were so relieved then, as the trailer was very drafty and cold. We slept there most nights and especially so during most of the Ardennes offensive, as casualties then were very high and more razias were conducted to round up men to help with the war effort. During that time we had no electricity, radio or newspapers. It felt like everything in The Netherlands came to a standstill except for the endless moving columns of German soldiers and armored vehicles. There was a curfew from sunset until sunrise. Everyone caught outside during that time was shot, no questions asked.

There were a lot of people in worse conditions than we were. We at least had bread to eat. We traded a lot of bread for vegetables and other edibles that neighbor farmers were able to eke out of the land. Kind people helped one another as much as they could. For some, though, there was little or no help at all.

War atrocities I witnessed

At different times throughout the war years I saw groups of Jews comprised of all ages, families included, carrying suitcases and other belongings being forced to march in the gutter side of the sidewalks. At their side, walking on the sidewalks, were the German soldiers with their guns at the ready. Alongside them or sometimes at the other side there was an army chaplain trying to calm the people and keep them moving forward. In a sanctimonious voice he would tell them to keep moving and that soon they would reach their destination in Eastern Europe where they would be resettled. There, they were told, each family would get a plot of land where they could grow their own potatoes. The chaplain would urge them to maintain good order and to keep pace.

As they passed in front of the houses facing the street, one could see some curtains moving. A few of the residents, like Mr. Blendheim, would pull the black-out curtains down so as not to see what was going on.

One time some kids and I followed one such group from a distance away as we were afraid of the soldiers. We came to the railroad station, and there it was a most confusing scene we could ever have imagined. The soldiers were pushing and shoving the people into the boxcars of a long train stationed there. There was a lot of shouting. "Snell, Snell". It seemed to me that everything had to be done on the double so that the people had no time to think. I saw a young mother with a baby in her arms trying to comfort her other two young ones that were crying. They were shoved into the boxcar. Amidst the noisy confusion I heard a little boy screaming:" Papa, Papa" Where was his papa, I wondered. I didn't see anyone there to pick him up or to comfort him. He too was shoved into the boxcar. I saw an old lady with a cane and she could hardly walk. The soldiers were shouting at her to keep moving. Finally one soldier grabbed her and very roughly shoved her into the boxcar. As he did this, her cane fell to the ground. When a small boy tried to pick the cane up for her, a soldier hit him in the head with the butt of his gun. The child screamed as blood ran from his head. Then the soldier kicked the cane under the train. The boy was pushed into the boxcar. I hoped he was all right. I remember wondering what the old lady would do in Eastern Europe without her cane. Little did we know most of them would die in a concentration camp, if they made it there, as some would die during the transport due to the terrible conditions they had to endure being jammed in like cattle, without food or water or sanitary facilities.

After the boxcars were crammed full with all the people, the doors were slammed shut and locked. The beer-bellied chaplain with his double chin and two Wehrmacht officers walked to a camouflage painted Army vehicle. One of the officers produced a bottle of schnapps. They all proceeded to drink from it. The chaplain then slapped his breeches with his hand and with a loud voice bragged "how they had sent another load of that Jewish vermin with a one way ticket to Walhalla (the Teutonic heaven)." It was very obvious then, that he knew the final destination of these poor people, and that he had lied to them.

Conditions rapidly deteriorated as the war went on. In the early winter of 1944 a lot of people were starving to death. At our bakery we could not longer bake every day as it was the custom, due to the severe rationing of grain and other foodstuffs. There was a shortage of everything including fuel wood. We were always hunting for wood to fire our ovens. We were able to locate some wood at a farm located about one hour walk away. One day I went there when there was a lull in the fighting, and the farmer loaded my pushcart with wood piled real high. It was not easy to push the cart along, and I was complaining about the size of the pile of wood. What I didn't realize was that the height of the load of wood would save my life. As I was pushing the precious cargo along, with a lot of effort, I came to a cluster of chestnut trees. Under one of the trees there was a military makeshift first aid station, where a medic was tending to some wounded soldiers. There was a chaplain there also, probably to give the last rites to some of the soldiers.

Unexpectedly the artillery shelling started. There was a big explosion as an Allied shell hit a heavy thick branch of the tree. The shell killed the medic who was attending two wounded soldiers. The two wounded soldiers had been in battle before as their uniforms were decorated with an iron cross first class. Amidst the screams, moans and groans, the chaplain who was standing at the right side of the tree was protected from the explosion by the trees' massive trunk He started shouting: "Shoot all these Americans S.O.B's! Shoot the American Schwein hunden"!

I was close enough to hear the chaplain cursing. So close that I would have been killed by the shrapnel that flew all around my cart. The high pile of wood served as a shield for me, and now I was grateful for the load I had to push. As there was nothing I could do to help out the soldiers, I walked on with my cart that somehow didn't feel so heavy anymore. I started wondering about the chaplain. Like most of the chaplains he was pretty hefty, with a double chin. Most of them, due to the privileged status they had did not have to look for food as the rest of the people had to do. Most of the civilians and the soldiers were very thin and haggard looking. The chaplains certainly did not go hungry. I wondered: Were they really representing God? I thought of the preacher of the Dutch Reformed Church that had given his sermon the Sunday before. He praised Hitler as God's wise appointed leader over the beloved German people. He even indicated that God himself would be wearing a party swastika armband like the one he was wearing. He said that God was marching alongside the German columns of faithful soldiers. The congregation broke out in applause. Was he a man of God? I wondered.

Continuing pushing my cart on the way back to the bakery I passed several other large chestnut trees. Then I came to a most gruesome sight. At the lower branch of one of the largest trees was hanging the body of a young German soldier, dressed in a Wehrmacht uniform. His hands were tied behind his back. His face was distorted, yet young looking, He looked like he was maybe 15 or 16 years old. On his boots there was a piece of cardboard with the word "DESERTER", in capital letters, written on it.

That sight made me sick. My cart now seemed heavier than usual. That boy was maybe my own age. Did he have a mother, a father and siblings waiting for his safe return at home? Was there a chaplain there to administer his last rites? Or, one that would have intervened on his behalf? No wonder that many Europeans lost their faith in God during that conflict. War is brutal and inhumane. Yet religious leaders blessed both sides of the War, with the outcome that Catholics were killing Catholics and Protestants were killing their fellow believers and all thinking they had the approval of God. I did not lose my faith in God, but I did lose my faith in organized religion. Something had gone terribly wrong with the teachings of the so-called "Christian" churches. From the little knowledge I had from the Bible, I just knew that what was happening could not be the results of the teachings of Christ and certainly could not have the approval of God. I did develop an aversion to the clergy from the Catholic and the Protestant denominations.

A stove for aunt Sjoertie

For years my aunt Sjoertie van der Starre was hiding her son who was 15 years old when the War started. He was born with Down's syndrome. She knew that the boy would be marked for the extermination camp as one whom the Nazis called "a useless eater". Aunt Sjoertie tried to eke out a modest living by selling groceries. However, during the cold and gloomy winter of 1944-1945 there was nothing to sell. They were living now in dire poverty. Our family tried to help with food. Now though, she didn't have a heating/cooking stove. Her old stove had cracked and was useless. There was nothing to be found made of metal in the whole country. All the iron, copper and metal goods were confiscated by the Germans, including the churches bells, to be sent to help with the war effort. Everything was melted for the making of war implements. My brother Joost and I were sleeping in a dilapidated utility trailer that was cold and drafty, to escape the searches by the German soldiers. They were looking for young men to be sent to Germany to work in the armament factories. We had an idea of what poor Aunt Sjoertie was going through. Worse yet, she could not cook the meager food we brought her. There was absolutely no way to buy or barter to get her a stove, not even an old one.

Joost, my brother, and I discussed many times how to help our aunt. We knew that the only way to get her a stove would be to steal one from the German army. We had watched many times the trains that carried the "flying-bombs" or V-rockets to the coast of Holland. They shot those rockets over the North Sea to England, particularly aiming at London. We could hear the heavy rumble, thunder-like of the rockets as they flew at night and see the long plume of light. Often the Germans had several heavily camouflaged rail cars loaded with the secret rockets waiting at a small station in Waddinxveen while they were preparing the launching site. The site was called "Sper-gebied", meaning that it was a restricted secret military area. It was located between Voorburg, The Hague, and Scheeveningen. The V-rockets were silver colored cylinders of about 15 meters long. A young German sentry with his gun at the ready would walk all around the train to protect its secret cargo. At the end of the train there was a caboose with a chimney sticking out of the roof. In the winter there was smoke coming out of the chimney, so we knew there was a heating stove there.

We began to observe closely the Germans and their routine. In order for the allied reconnaissance pilots not to spot the trains these were camouflaged with a netting of greenish-gray colored thick ropes. The trains were moved under the cover of night darkness, via Gouda, to the restricted area, so as to avoid detection. Once parked there, we noticed that there was a change of the sentry guard every two hours. At the change of the guard, an Obergefreiter (corporal) came with the relief sentry. The Obergefreiter would shout a few commands in the German language. The sentry who was on guard duty, the new relief guard and the corporal would all click the heels of their hobnailed boots. They would raise their right arm and shout "Heil Hitler". Then both guards would make a few goose steps toward each other. They would click their boots again and the sentry that was just relieved would march under the watchful eye of the Obergefreiter back to the Beukenhof (a home that they had taken over for their quarters), a distance of about a quarter mile away. The new sentry now made his way marching around the train, and we timed this carefully.

At the next change of guard we quietly and furtively made our way to the caboose. Inside it we observed that there were 2 chairs and a small table with an extra helmet on it. There was also a small cabinet and two single bunk beds. Above one bunk bed there was a 10x12 picture of Adolf Hitler in a Wehrmacht uniform with an Iron Cross on his chest. The slogan underneath the picture stated: "The Fuhrer watches over you".

Above the other bunk bed there was a picture of Joseph Goebbels, and the slogan underneath it said: "In this lodge anything is likely to take place, with one exception: that we capitulate". Goebbels was adept at inventing Nazi slogans. I remember many of them. One that stuck in my mind as a child was: "Attention Germanic soldiers: the enemy is always listening in on all your conversations". We were now trying to listen to the sound of the marching boots of the sentry. As we looked around, something startled us. Next to the door of the caboose an extra long field gray German army trench coat was hanging on a hook. We knew it did not belong to the sentry, because it had the markings of a Feldwebel (sergeant) and the sentry was a Gefreiter (soldier first class). That gave us an uneasy feeling. It was like a menacing shadow over our plan. Even now I can easily see that coat. We had calculated we had to deal with only one sentry. We almost ran out. However as we turned around we saw what we came for. There it was: a small iron stove with glowing coals inside. It stood on a small square platform that stood about 6 inches from the wooden floor and it was bolted to it on 4 sides. However the stove was bolted to the platform with only 3 bolts. Of these, one was missing. We knew that we only had to loosen two bolts. That would surely save us time. We heard the sentry approaching on the other side. We quickly jumped out before he could march around outside the caboose on our side, and we quietly hid under the train behind the double iron wheels on the opposite side. The sentry went inside the caboose to warm himself. Without making a sound we left our hiding place and ran home. There we got a wrench, a short iron crowbar and old rags and gunny sacks to handle the hot stove.

Back at our hiding place close to the train, we waited for almost two hours for the next change of guard. Then, we quickly and quietly entered the caboose. To our despair, as we tried to loosen the nuts that held the stove to the little platform, we found out they were rusted to the bolts. It would take a much longer time for us to free the stove.

We were prepared to surprise the sentry in case of confrontation. That was the reason for us to bring the crowbar along. The sentry looked like he was just about my age, a teenager, maybe 15 or 16 years old. Fortunately we did not have to resort to violence to defend ourselves. As we heard him approaching, we were able to hide again behind the iron wheels underneath the train. When he returned to his round, we went back to our job and finally were able to remove the nuts from the bolts. We had to go back into hiding again as we listened to the thump-thump of the guard's boots.

The sentry went inside the caboose to warm himself, but this time he stayed a much longer time. We were worried that he would notice that the nuts of the bolts were gone, or that he would notice something else out of the ordinary. We did not feel the cold, as we were perspiring with fear.

Finally he left for his next round. We stealthily entered the caboose and by using the gunny sack and the old rags we first removed the section of the stove pipe above the elbow that connected the pipe to the stove. Then we lifted the stove from its moorings and holding it between us with the sacks and the rags, we took it outside. We walked as fast as we could, almost running. The rags were not a match for the heat of the stove. It also was heavier than we thought. So we had to put it down several times as we walked.

It was getting dark now. As we rested one more time, heading toward the edge of the forest, we looked back. To our horror we saw that every time we rested, there was a dark, burned round area on the ground from the bottom of the hot stove.

We knew that the sentry would not be able to leave his guard duty to come after us, as the precious cargo of the train, the V-rockets, was more important than an old stove. He would have to wait for the next change of guard. But now they would have a trail to follow.

My brother and I looked at each other. Should we abandon the stove and run? Then, I felt something wet on my face. I looked up. Snowflakes! Big ones! More and more! They started to come down real fast. The ground would soon be covered with the snow! The snow and the darkness of the night would obliterate our tracks. With renewed energy we ran. Reaching the cover of the trees, our hearts pounding, we never stopped until we reached our aunt's home.

At aunt Sjoertie's house we found out that installing the stove was a lot harder than stealing it. Her home had a brick chimney. The hole in the chimney was too high. We needed another piece of stove pipe, which we knew would have been impossible to purchase anywhere. We also did not want to go back to the rail yard to steal the pipe. The platform that our aunt had for the old stove was broken and totally unusable. We had to improvise somehow. We took one of her wooden chairs and sawed the back off. We had to make a fire-proof or fire resistant platform. Measuring everything carefully we realized that we had to evenly cut a few inches of the four legs of the chair. Then we placed the four bricks of the old platform on the top of the chair. Aunt Sjoertie had an old galvanized tub with a lid on it. We took the lid and placed it on the top of the four bricks. The stove was placed on the top of this contraption and hooked up to the brick chimney. The whole thing looked very amusing to me. It really was not a pretty sight to see, but it would serve its purpose. We placed the leftover wood of the chair in the stove and we could feel the warm glow of the heat. We looked at our aunt. This was the very first time I had seen her smile. I never remember her smiling before. Because of the heavy emotional burden she had, she always walked around with a frown on her face. Her radiant face now lit up the room. That facial expression alone was the best payment we could ever ask for. It was worth all the work and the risks we went thru. No inflation could diminish that investment.

Aunt Sjoertie insisted that my brother and I would eat with her and her son. The problem now was that she had only three chairs for her table. She made us and her son sit on the chairs and she turned over the galvanized tub that lost its lid for the stove, and used it to sit on. I will never forget the simple meal we had. My brother and I were famished, as we had no time to eat the whole day. We were busy getting a stove. In front of us she placed a small ceramic bowl of cooked mashed rutabagas. There were only three ceramic bowls. She used an old coffee mug for herself. She had nothing else. Since she was hiding her handicapped son, she could get only one ration card. Also, during the winter of 1944 there was no salt, sugar, or any spices to be found anywhere. A lot of people were starving and many, including children, died of hunger. Dogs and cats disappeared. Anything edible was consumed, including tulip bulbs. Aunt Sjoertie had sold almost everything in the house she could. That was why her house was so sparsely furnished. How she survived with her son thru the war was just short of a miracle. When she could she would pick chestnuts from the trees that were around in the area. She also would dig for the dark brown tuberous underground fungus. Yet that winter she could only find rutabagas. She apologized that she could not make them taste better for the lack of salt and spices. Before we could eat she bowed her head and said a prayer thanking God for the stove and for the meal we were about to partake.

Before that winter my aunt would cook the rutabagas with some of the sugar beets we were able to provide for her. Or she would cook them with some chopped tulip bulbs, and maybe even chestnuts from the chestnuts trees nearby. Now, though, because of the tough cold weather, foodstuffs were very sparse. As insipid as that meal was, we were grateful to have something in our stomachs. After we left, though, my brother who had become very irreligious as he saw people of the same faith on both sides of the war killing each other while both sides were praying to God for the victory, said: "That was not much of a meal to give thanks for, was it?"

As we walked back, thru the frosty grass fields in the dark of night, to the abandoned, deteriorating, cold and drafty utility trailer that served as our sleeping quarters, we avoided the road so as not to be detected by any German patrols as we were way past the curfew time. Thankfully it was still snowing and the snow would cover over any tracks. We pondered over many questions we had for which the clergy were not able to give us a satisfactory answer. Why were Christians on both sides of the war killing one another and praying to God for the victory? Why were members of the same church, like in our own family so divided by politics and national issues? What happened to the love of Christ? Why would some think that the Jews of this generation had to be persecuted for being Christ's killers when Jesus himself had forgiven the ones that actually did it?

Back at the trailer, I started complaining about the cold. We had placed straw on the floor and plugged many holes with gunny sacks, yet we could not make any improvements like covering up the little window that was broken. It was the only window the trailer had. However, if we had made changes that would be visible on the outside, that would bring the German patrols to inspect the place to see if it was occupied. Joost, my brother, reminded me of the paucity of aunt Sjoertie's life, and that she never complained, and she was thankful if only for a scoop of tasteless rutabagas. Because of what he had seen thru the war he was almost an atheist. Yet he had outstanding human qualities. He was a lot more humane than many pro-Hitler clergymen we had seen with a cross around their necks and with a pretentious piety on their demeanor.

To preserve the so-called Germanic supremacy, Hitler declared that anyone with genetic defects, or whom he considered to be racially or genetically inferior, and the ones he called "useless eaters", should be eliminated. Many German scientists and clergymen supported Hitler's policy of the "purification" of the Germanic race. The ones they thought of "unfit" or "untermenschen"(sub-humans) had to be exterminated. This program was openly talked about and it was labeled "merciful elimination of the unfit". We personally heard clergymen giving their support to Hitler's policies. I clearly remember going to a Sunday service and the preacher of the Reformed Church whose name was Vroegindewij thanking God for placing such a wise and highly skilled leader, Adolph Hitler over God's beloved Germanic people. Right after the war as I walked past the same church, thru an open window I heard the same preacher thanking God for the Allied victory.

Every German soldier had a chain with a cross around his neck. In their belt buckle the inscription was: "Gott mit uns"("God is with us"). Under those insignias they drove millions of innocent victims to the gas chambers. Most of the clergy supported Hitler's policies and some had a general "just go along" policy. Rarely a few showed their opposition to the regime, especially at the beginning of the war. Toward the end, because of the oppressiveness and suffering, and because the Germans were losing on many fronts, some clergymen switched sides.

During the war, there was so-called "freedom of worship", yet not freedom of religion. You were free to worship at any church that had signed an agreement with Hitler. Jehovah's Witnesses never compromised with Hitler. So they were terribly persecuted. Jews and Gypsies never had a chance. They and Jehovah's Witnesses were forbidden to practice their religion. The Witnesses went underground and had their meetings secretly. I personally knew an old man that refused to say "Heil Hitler" as a greeting. At the time I did not know why. The Gestapo arrested him and sent him to the Westerbork concentration camp. After the war I learned he was one of the Jehovah's Witnesses. The Jews had to wear a yellow Star of David on their clothing. I saw rows of them marched in the gutters, as they were not allowed to walk on the sidewalks. They were herded to the concentration camps. One time I saw the Gestapo herding a family and a few young men. They had no markings on their clothes. They did not look down dejectedly. I wondered who they were. I was told these were the hated Bible students. I also learned later that they were Jehovah's Witnesses who were known as International Bible Students. Little did I know one day I would be one of them.

My brother and I felt very bad for the suffering of so many innocent ones. We became more determined to help our aunt and her son. We did more ice-fishing. During that winter even the fish were scarce and hard to find. The ones we usually threw back in the water, like bony mud bass or the spiny stickling bass, were now precious. What a treat for the hungry to have fish soup made out of them, head and all. In the spring our aunt would throw dandelions into the soup and/or any other greens she could find. Some people cooked any grasses they could find. Young and old were starving to death.

It was remarkable that our aunt Sjoertie survived the war with her son. Many people who were hiding handicapped ones, or other unfortunate ones like the Jews, were denounced by their so-called Christian neighbors. The Nazis offered generous bounties to anyone who would bring into the open the ones that were hidden for their so-called racial inferiority, forbidden religious practices, genetic defects, or for any considered "useless eaters". There was an atmosphere of distrust and neighbor feared neighbor. One had to be extremely careful; otherwise one could be denounced as an enemy of the State. The consequences were dire. Due to the political division in our own family my brother and I could not reveal to any of them what we had done to help our aunt. She did not know where her stove came from, yet wisely she never asked. The secret remained with my brother and me for many, many years.

The Gestapo was very proficient in tracing people down. Another reason that we escaped from being apprehended for stealing a hot stove right under the noses of the German army was an incredible coincidence. My brother Joost and I picked the right day, unknowingly of course, to help our aunt. It was the opening day of the Ardennes offensive, the battle of the Bulge. That surprise attack on the Allies took precedent over everything. A missing hot stove would now take the back burner. They had other priorities on their mind.

Like so many in those days, my aunt lived a very arduous life, full of deprivations. She was so devoted to her son that many times when there was just a little food left, she went hungry in order for him to have something to eat. She always looked sad and gloomy, yet never complained. Her son lived until the summer of 1951. Shortly after his death she passed away also. The light of her life had gone out. The terrible war years took a heavy toll on many that survived, as it did shorten their lives afterwards, due to the physical deprivations and the emotional and psychological trauma they endured.

Shortly after the war I had a terrible reminder of the hot stove incident. This I describe in the next chapter: "The graveside in Niederlahnstein".

The graveside in Niederlahnstein

On a sunny morning, right after the war, I was walking in the area where the Lahn River empties itself into the Rhine River, close to a small German town called Niederlahnstein. Walking up a hill I came to a cemetery where quite a few German soldiers were buried. One of the graves got my attention. There on a gravestone, behind a glass frame was a picture of a young soldier, maybe 15 or 16 years old. On his uniform there was a "V" embroidered in silver thread. This meant his rank was of "gefreiter" (soldier first class). The face in that picture looked vaguely familiar.

That encounter sent a shiver up my spine. Was he the same sentry that guarded the train when my brother and I stole the stove from the caboose? We never thought of the consequences to the sentry or to any other guards of that train. Underneath the photograph these words were carved on the stone: "Remember my beloved son." I sat down beside the grave and wept.

This young man as well as any others had mothers and fathers, siblings or other members of the family waiting for them to come back home, and they never did. War causes sufferings and anguish to either side of the conflict. Calling the other side "enemies" dehumanizes them and it makes people ready to kill one another. How quickly they forget Jesus' words: "Love thy enemy" (Matthew 5:44).

As I sat besides that grave, I remembered that when the Germans had invaded Holland, I was walking close to our home and I saw a German soldier sitting by the sidewalk. He looked at me and his face turned very sad. He motioned for me to come closer and when I did, he took out his wallet. From his wallet he took out a photograph of a young boy. When I looked at the picture I was astonished on how this boy looked just like me. The soldier, with tears in his eyes pointed to the picture and said: "My son". Then I understood "this enemy" was a human also, with feelings just like me. I felt very sad for him. As I walked home, I looked back and I saw this soldier kissing the picture of his son.

At the grave at Niederlahnstein I also pondered about what was going on back in The Netherlands. When the war came to an end, there was great jubilation. However, not long after that, a spirit of revenge enveloped a great number of the population. Not many like to talk about it now. But it did happen. Lots of people became preoccupied with taking revenge on their countrymen who were sympathizers with the Nazi regime. Many were tortured and killed at that time. Homes of Nazi sympathizers were looted. Everything they had was taken away. Some were thrown in jails, some were tortured, and some were killed, including their children. Mobs were formed and guilty and innocent ones were severely beaten. The women who had befriended German soldiers, whether they did it for their own survival, or not, were singled out and after they were beaten they were made to sit on high chairs and then they had their hair shaven off in a very rough manner. The crowd would jeer, laugh loudly and scream at them with abusive terms. Most applauded to show their approval.

Coincidentally, at the same place where I witnessed some of these women having their heads shaved, I witnessed another terrible episode when the Germans were still occupying the Netherlands.

As I mentioned before, the Jews had to wear a yellow Star of David on their clothing to identify them as being Jews. They had to walk in the gutter along the sidewalk. This one time I was walking on the Kerkweg (Church Street) that had only one sidewalk, on the east side. On the other side there was a canal. An old Jewish man was walking South in the gutter of that street. I think he was a Rabbi or a teacher of some sort, because of the orthodox clothes he was wearing. He also had a long beard and side locks.

A company of German soldiers were marching North on the same street. When they met the old man the Oberst shouted for his troop to halt. Then he shouted for them to make a turn to face him and to stand at ease. The Oberst grabbed the old man and beat him. He knocked the eye-glasses off the old man and stomped on them with his boots. Then he ripped the tassels and some of the apparel of the old man's orthodox clothes and threw them in the gutter. He made the old man sit on a broken down brick wall. With his bayonet the Oberst sheared the beard and the side locks of the old man. He did it so brutally, that the blood ran from his head and chin. Every time the old man did scream, the Oberst would shout: "Shut up you cursed dirty Jewish swine".

There was a crowd now watching. The Oberst made the old man stand in front of the whole company of soldiers. Turning to the soldiers and then to the crowd, the Oberst gloatingly asked: "You brave soldiers of our Great Third Reich, and you good Dutch people of pure Germanic blood:—How do you like the way I cleaned up this dirty Jewish swine?" All of the soldiers applauded in approval and so did most of the crowd. Only a few stared disapprovingly.

Did the ones that applauded do so because they were intimidated, or because of the peer pressure? Did the few that disapproved then, later approved of the shaving and the brutal treatment of the women after the war? From what I saw I learned that violence begets violence, and it can turn into a vicious circle that never ends.

All those things I pondered about sitting next to that Niederlahnstein grave. I had many questions now in my mind and afterwards I spent a great deal of time asking many religious leaders about my thoughts. None of them were capable of giving me a satisfactory answer. I was so glad later on, to learn from the Bible that revenge belongs to God. Only He can repay justly. (Romans 12:19). It is also a comfort to know that in the near future He will make wars to cease, as He promised in His Word, the Bible, at Isaiah 2:4 and Psalm 46:9.

After World War II there was great pressure in Europe to forget all of what did happen, especially the atrocities that both sides of the conflict experienced. People wanted to look to the future with new hopes and forget the past. Most churches clergy now preached total forgiveness and forgetfulness. However, in doing so there is a danger that history will be repeated. One can forgive, but in this case, one should not forget. Lessons need to be learned from what happened in that horrible time.

Some are trying to make believe that the atrocities of the Second World War never happened. Survivors are getting old and dying. They need to let their stories be known so that those in denial will not get the upper hand. Many today know that over six million Jews were annihilated in the Holocaust. How many though know about the annihilation of the victims of the Nuremberg law of racial purity? The ones that were called sub-humans due to genetic defects? Or how many remember the genocide of the European gypsies? How many know that the first prisoners in the concentration camps were Jehovah's Witnesses and how terribly they were treated, persecuted and killed for their faith? And that some of their young men were beheaded because they refused to kill their fellowmen from other Countries?

To forget is to excuse the hatred behind all these atrocities and many other injustices that occurred during the war time. By building a close relationship with our Creator we can learn to forgive and to find peace, like I did. But not even the Creator let us forget of the sins his own people committed. They were recorded in his book, the Bible so that we all can learn from their mistakes and try not to repeat them. Forgiveness is one thing. It can bring tranquility of mind. Forgetfulness is something totally different. It does not teach us not to repeat the same error again. We can and should learn from our mistakes.

How can I intermingle a bread book with my memories? For me they are interchangeable as I grew up baking bread in a time of war. I also found out that bread making is of therapeutic value. The steady rhythm of kneading the dough is very soothing. Punching the dough relieves one of anxiety and it helps to get rid of any frustration. It might help you also, as life in this system of things can be very frustrating at times. So go ahead, knead and punch your dough and you will feel much better. And then you will have the end result of wonderful loaves of bread that are truly satisfying.

Proverbs pertaining to our daily bread

The Dutch people love their proverbs. They have proverbs for almost everything. The following proverbs deal with: first, the quality of bread and second, the hard times of war and hunger. Underlying qualities and character of people shine through most of these proverbs. Some are traditional. Some are original.

In order to understand some of the proverbs there is a need to understand some of the colloquial expressions used by the Dutch people, for instance, the meaning of the expression Horse Bread.

In older times there was no commercial animal feed. Dogs and cats consumed scraps or leftovers from their owner's tables. Horses and cows and other animals were fed grains, besides the grasses of their pastures. Some people would feed a type of whole grain rye bread to their prized animals.

Usually every Monday our bakery would produce about 120 loaves of real heavy black bread that was made with rye and lots of wheat bran. The compact and dense loaves were known by various names. Some called them "servant's bread" and others "beggars bread". At the bakery we called it "Mondays Horse Bread", because some of our customers would feed their horses with it.

In those times eating refined white bread and delicate pastries was a status symbol. Some of the prosperous landowners would buy the rich white bread, cookies and pastries for themselves, and feed the peasants who worked for them the cheaper, coarse, dark grainy bread. In this way the color of the bread became associated with one's lot in life. The rich ate white bread and the poor the dark grainy bread. They did not realize that the poor were a lot healthier for it. Some of our wealthier customers would send the maid to buy our products, and because they did like the whole grain breads, they would advise the maid to always cover theirs baskets with a towel, or they had a special hamper with a lid on it, so that the neighbors would not see what kind of edibles they had purchased.

When the Germans invaded Holland, the rationing of food stuffs was started. The best of foods was sent to Germany. The refined white bread became a rarity. I remember one of the wealthy burghers coming to our shop and not finding his favorite white bread became irate and said: "Civilized, cultured people eat only white bread. This despicable black coarse bread is for the horses". I replied: "That it is why the horses have the stamina and the strength to run with the civilized people on their backs". I hoped he got the point that the whole grain loaves were a lot healthier than the refined white ones. Those loaves were fat-free, had no sugar and were very low in sodium chlorine. In today's world, health conscious people pay a premium for such healthy bread. How things have changed!

The reason for this explanation is that it will make it easier to understand some of the proverbs that follow. The color of the bread in the olden days signified the station in life that a person had. "Horse bread" was for the peasants. The rich consumed refined white bread.

- Bread stops an old horse from kicking backward.
- A good horse is worth his rye bread.
- A horse doesn't see the color of his bread.
- Bread is for the work horse. The whip is for the lazy one.
- Good dough is not bread.
- Everyone butter his bread his own way.
- He is not worthy of the salt in his bread.
- Bread is better than gold.
- Bread, cheese and wine are a delight to the soul.
- A banquet without bread is like a king without a crown.
- If your bread box is empty, they rather see your heels than your toes.

- The smaller the bread, the quicker it will bake.
- Money does much. Bread does it most.
- When there is no bread, lentils become a luxury.
- Wisdom is better than bread.
- Bread is just as good at one end as it is at the other.
- Flour is good but bread is better.
- Gold is better than silver, yet bread is better than both.
- One pound of bread is better than two pounds of dough.
- Sourdough makes the bread what it is.
- Some speeches are as tasteless as salt free bread.
- Bread is to a man what sunshine is to a harvest.
- Bread and butter are a heavenly match.
- Better to have bread on the table than a fattened calf in the stable.
- Bread is made to share. It shows that you do care.
- A loaf of bread and a stein of beer can be good health restorers.
- Some people's bread is not worth remembering.
- Old bread needs more butter.
- The early customer has the choice of the bread.
- Better old dry bread in honor than fresh bread and butter in shame.
- Bad grain can only produce bad bread.
- Sometimes good bread will divide the best of friends.
- Bread can bring people together, yet bread can also separate one from another.
- The worse the flour, the worse the bread.
- Breaking bread together can make friendships last.
- Some have hope. Others have bread.
- Hold back your bread before you know you have a true friend.
- There are some that complain of hunger with a stomach full of bread.
- Bread can bring both: quarreling and peace.
- You can make more friends with bread than you can with vinegar.
- Bread upon the table of the poor is more appreciated than the meat upon the table of the rich.
- A fool will complain even if God himself would rain down bread from the heaven.

- When the hand ceases to pass the bread around, the mouth ceases to praise the giver.
- When the lazy is short of bread he blames his misfortune.
- To the one bread with butter is despised. To the other dry bread is a luxury.
- Some get free bread, but they are too lazy to break it.
- The beggar asks for bread but is hoping for a steak.
- When the belly of the pig is full he will trample on buttered bread.
- The bread basket of the lazy is bottomless.
- He who marries a fool for his bread will lose the bread and keep the fool.
- Give bread to a foolish beggar and he will judge its color.
- When eating bread at your neighbor's house do not discuss the color of the loaf.
- Due to circumstances, sometimes even the most underserving ones eat the best of bread.
- You never know how the bread looks like until you open the oven door.
- There are always the ones that are the first in cutting the bread and the last to leave the table.
- If you eat your bread by the glow of a low candle you will not see the color of the loaf.
- It's better to be slow in taking the bread out of the oven than to burn your fingers.
- A meal of sweet bread is delicious. Sweet bread for every meal is nauseating.
- You cannot get a sour stomach from bread that you never ate.
- In times of prosperity a lot of people forget to pray for their daily bread.
- After the baking is done you cannot improve the loaf.
- Dreaming of bread does not fill the stomach.
- One that has plenty of bread is usually listened to; the one that lacks bread is often ignored.
- There is more culture in Flemish bread than there is in Flemish beer.
- Beer, cheese and bread are worthy of the extra sweat.
- It is easy to give bigger chunks of bread from someone else's loaf.

- Some people earn their bread with ease and the butter comes as they please.
- Give bread away and you will make friends. Ask for payment and you will make enemies.
- Better a little bread in peace than lots of it in discontent.
- Sooner or later any bread box will be empty.
- Good bread will not change bad manners.
- Speaking is worth the bread. Listening is worth the bread and butter.
- For good bread we endure the oven's heat.
- Two things are impossible to fill: a bottomless basket and the bread box of the lazy one.
- Two things that never say:" It's enough"—a fishnet with a big hole in it and the lazy one's crying for bread.
- The stomach of the lazy one is forever empty, while the diligent one eats bread to satisfaction.
- The diligent ones will always have bread while the slack ones will go hungry.
- A true friend will share his bread with his companion in his hour of need.
- Every baker thinks his bread is cake.
- In the kingdom of bread and cheese there is no need for hunger to appease.
- Bread and beer are good servants but make bad masters.
- Where bread paves the way, butter and cheese follow.
- If you give to some a slice of bread they will take the whole loaf.
- You will not save the bread with fasting.
- It is a very sad thing to enter a bakery with an empty stomach and an empty wallet as well.
- Never eat bread before it is thoroughly baked.
- You cannot eat two loaves of bread at once.
- Good bread is less what you see, more what you taste.
- Never cut your bread before it is baked.
- Better a small meal with bread than a large one without it.
- Not everyone that wears a baker's hat knows how to bake good bread.
- Flattery seldom puts bread on the table.
- Better a bread giver than an advice giver.

- Bread is a universal food. It will be there wherever you go.
- Bread is unique. It will always taste after its own oven.
- Bread will never go out of style.
- He who has bread will find a knife to cut it.
- Choose your friends before you share your bread.
- No one eats bread with a spoon.
- The miser will die of hunger with a full bread box.
- A jealous person will call other people's sweetest bread sour.
- The crust is also bread. Sometimes the best part of the bread.
- For the lack of bread many wars were started.
- Why ask for butter when there is no bread?
- The bread of the diligent one is always buttered.
- Be wary of people who know which side of the bread is buttered before you butter it.
- There will always be givers and takers. Givers will share their bread with others. Takers expect others to share their bread with them.
- A peasant with bread is in better position than a hungry king.
- Sometimes a man is praised in proportion to the size of his bread box.
- There always will be the ones that will charm the others out of their bread.
- There is no end to writing proverbs about bread. Better stop now.

Introduction to White Breads

Baking good white bread starts with the buying of good quality white flour. The texture and the flavor of the bread are to a great extent determined by the quality of the flour used. The quality of the flour plays a much bigger role and it is far more important than any other ingredient you add to the dough. You may add the best of any other ingredient to your dough, yet if the flour is of a poor quality, this will be reflected on the final product. For best results, use good quality all-purpose unbleached flour.

If you are a novice on bread making, it is best to start with a simple recipe and then as you get practice, to move on to more complex techniques. Some of the richer white bread recipes will call for more experienced bakers to produce delightful loaves. The more you work at it, the more successful you will be at the very satisfying and rewarding experience of bread baking.

When it comes to bread, there is no end to experimentation. There is an infinity variety in the shapes and the ingredients of the loaves. There is fun in trying different ways and methods, including ethnic and international recipes. It is a satisfying and rewarding experience. For me there is nothing better than the aroma of freshly baked bread in a home. It does give you a feeling of accomplishment, joy and satisfaction when you see your family and friends enjoying the work of your hands. May many compliments go your way!

If you cannot make your own bread, it does pay to get a good product. Good bread is worth the extra money. I remember a trip through Simco, Ontario, Canada where my wife and I stopped at a small bakery operated by a French Canadian couple. At the counter there was a British couple loudly complaining about the price of the bread. They were well groomed and had a prosperous appearance. The man was smoking a long stemmed pipe which he held with one hand and in the other hand he held a long leash that was attached to a dachshund. They left without purchasing anything. I remembered thinking to myself that I would rather spend the money on good bread than on tobacco. My wife and I had purchased some apple bread and two cups of coffee and went to sit outside where there were some tables and chairs. As we were enjoying our repast, lo and behold, the British couple came back. They went inside, bought some coffee and came out, sitting next to us. Then they unpacked the commercial bread they purchased at a local supermarket. After eating a slice of the commercial bread, they started talking to us. I then let them try a slice of the apple bread we were enjoying. Well, one look at their faces, and they went back to the small bakery and got some of the apple bread to enjoy with their coffee. They could have saved the money that they spent on the commercial loaf. Well, maybe the dog ate it afterwards, and perhaps got constipated.

It was very obvious that the French Canadian baker had a passion for excellence. Good quality bread will sell itself.

There is nothing better though, than homemade bread. It has such a wonderful taste and texture that it is hard to duplicate in mass production. So, let's start with a few recipes of white bread and may you enjoy the delectable results.

Crusty French Bread

This bread was a favorite of the rich Dutch burghers before and after the Second World War. When you savor it you will know why. It is delicious with some Brie cheese and a glass of red wine. It is crusty on the outside, yet soft and chewy on the inside. There are many recipes for French bread on the market. This one is exceptionally flavorful and crusty, and to my opinion it beats all others

Ingredients:

- 1 tablespoon dry yeast.
- 2 cups warm (110°F) water.
- Approximately 6 cups unbleached all-purpose flour.
- 3 egg whites, at room temperature, lightly beaten. Reserve 1 tablespoon egg white for glazing.
- 1 teaspoon salt.

Yield: 4 small long loaves.

In a 6-quart mixing bowl, dissolve half of the yeast in 1 cup of the water. Add 1 cup of the flour. Mix well. Let this mixture ferment in a warm (75°F) place for 4 hours.

After the 4 hours, add to the mixture the rest of the yeast and the water. Mix well.

Add the remaining ingredients and work them into dough.

Turn the dough out onto a lightly floured surface and knead it for 7 minutes until it is smooth and elastic. Return the dough to the mixing bowl and cover it with a towel. Let the dough rise in a warm place for 1 hour, or until it is doubled in bulk.

Divide the dough into 4 equal parts. Shape each part into a long loaf about 12 inches long. Set the loaves on a large baking sheet that has been liberally dusted with cornmeal. Cover the loaves with a towel and let them rise again in a warm place for 40 minutes.

Score the loaves with 4 or 5 diagonal slashes made with a very sharp knife. Brush the loaves with a mixture of 1 tablespoon egg white and 1 tablespoon water.

Place the loaves in a pre-heated 400°F oven. After 3 minutes spray or brush the loaves with a little cold water so as to create extra steam. Close the oven door. After another 3 minutes spray or brush with a little cold water again. Finish baking for about 24 to 25 minutes or until golden brown. If you like the loaves to be extra crunchy turn the oven off and leave the loaves in the oven with the closed door for another 5 minutes.

With heat resistant gloves, remove the loaves from the oven and place them on a wire rack to allow them to cool off.

Cinnamon Bread

There is nothing like this flavorful bread to delight children and adults alike. It makes the house smell wonderfully as it is baking. It goes real well with butter and honey, or with a delicious fruit jam. It is just luscious when toasted.

Ingredients:

- 1 tablespoon dry yeast.
- 2 cups warm (110°F) milk.
- 2½ tablespoons sugar
- 2½ tablespoons soft butter
- 1½ teaspoons cinnamon
- 1 teaspoon salt
- Approximately 6 cups unbleached all-purpose flour.

Filling:

- Melted butter,
- 1 cup cinnamon sugar

Yield: 2 medium-size loaves.

In a 6 quart mixing bowl dissolve the yeast in the milk. Add the remaining ingredients and work them into dough.

Turn the dough out onto a lightly floured surface and knead it for about 7 minutes, until the dough is smooth and somewhat elastic.

Return the dough to the mixing bowl and cover it with a clean towel. Let the dough rise in a warm place for about 1 hour.

Divide the dough into 2 equal loaves. Flour your hands and flatten each loaf into a 12x8 rectangle. Brush the melted butter over each rectangle and sprinkle the cinnamon sugar over the melted butter. Fold the short side over and roll each rectangle as you would a jelly roll.

Charel Scheele

Set each loaf seam side down into a greased loaf pan. Cover the loaves with a towel. Let them rise for 45 minutes.

Bake the loaves in a preheated 390°F oven for about 40 minutes.

With heat resistant gloves, remove the loaves from the oven and let them cool on a wire rack.

Crusty Italian Bread

This bread is excellent for making sandwiches. It has a light texture and a nice chewy crust. It is a real treat when paired with cold cuts

Ingredients:

- 1 tablespoon dry yeast.
- 2 cups warm (110°F) water.
- Approximately 6 cups unbleached all-purpose flour.
- 1 egg white, at room temperature, lightly beaten.
- 1 teaspoon salt.

Yield: 2 medium-size loaves.

In a 6 quart mixing bowl dissolve the yeast in the water. Add the remaining ingredients and work them into dough.

Turn the dough out onto a lightly floured surface and knead it for about 7 minutes, until the dough is smooth and somewhat elastic.

Return the dough to the mixing bowl and cover it with a clean towel. Let the dough rise in a warm place for about 1 hour.

Divide the dough into 2 equal loaves. Flour your hands and flatten each loaf into a 12x8 rectangle. Fold the short side over to the center half of the rectangle. Then fold the other side over to overlap about a half and inch the first fold. Press flat again. Starting with the short end, tightly roll the rectangle into a loaf.

Set the loaves seam side down onto a greased baking sheet. Cover them with a towel and let the loaves rise for about 45 minutes in a warm place.

Bake the loaves in a preheated 390°F. oven for about 40 minutes.

With heat resistant gloves, remove the loaves from the oven and set them on a wire rack to cool off.

Egg Bread

Ingredients:

- 1 tablespoon dry yeast.
- 2 cups warm (110°F) milk
- 2 tablespoons sugar
- 1 tablespoon soft butter.
- Approximately 6 cups unbleached all-purpose flour.
- 2 large eggs at room temperature, lightly beaten.
- 1 teaspoon salt.

Yield: 2 medium-size loaves.

In a 6 quart mixing bowl dissolve the yeast in the milk. Add the remaining ingredients and work them into dough.

Turn the dough out onto a lightly floured surface and knead it for about 7 minutes, until the dough is smooth and somewhat elastic.

Return the dough to the mixing bowl and cover it with a clean towel. Let the dough rise in a warm place for about 1 hour.

Divide the dough into 2 equal halves. Flour your hands and flatten each half into a 12x8 rectangle. Fold the short side over to about half of the rectangle. Then fold the opposite side overlapping the first fold by about half an inch. Press flat again and starting from the short end roll the dough tightly into a loaf.

Set each loaf seam side down into a greased loaf pan. Cover the loaves with a towel. Let them rise for 45 minutes. Bake the loaves in a preheated 390°F oven for about 40 minutes. With heat resistant gloves, remove the loaves from the oven and let them cool on a wire rack.

White Bread

Ingredients:

- 1 tablespoon dry yeast.
- 2 cups warm (110°F) water.
- ½ stick (2oz.) soft butter
- ½ cup sugar
- Approximately 6 cups unbleached all-purpose flour.
- 1 teaspoon salt.

Yield: 2 medium-size loaves.

In a 6 quart mixing bowl dissolve the yeast in the water. Add the remaining ingredients and work them into dough.

Turn the dough out onto a lightly floured surface and knead it for about 7 minutes, until the dough is smooth and somewhat elastic.

Return the dough to the mixing bowl and cover it with a clean towel. Let the dough rise in a warm place for about 1 hour.

Divide the dough into 2 equal halves. Flour your hands and flatten each half into a 12x8 rectangle. Fold the short side over to about half of the rectangle. Then fold the opposite side overlapping the first fold by about half an inch. Press flat again and starting from the short end roll the dough tightly into a loaf.

Set each loaf seam side down into a greased loaf pan. Cover the loaves with a towel. Let them rise for 45 minutes.

Bake the loaves in a preheated 390°F oven for about 40 minutes. With heat resistant gloves, remove the loaves from the oven and let them cool on a wire rack.

Potato Bread

Ingredients:

- 1 tablespoon dry yeast.
- 2 cups warm (110°F) water.
- 2 tablespoons soft butter
- ½ cup dry potato flakes
- 2 tablespoon sugar
- Approximately 6 cups unbleached all-purpose flour.
- 1 teaspoon salt.

Yield: 2 medium-size loaves.

In a 6 quart mixing bowl dissolve the yeast in the water. Add the remaining ingredients and work them into dough.

Turn the dough out onto a lightly floured surface and knead it for about 7 minutes, until the dough is smooth and somewhat elastic.

Return the dough to the mixing bowl and cover it with a clean towel. Let the dough rise in a warm place for about 1 hour.

Divide the dough into 2 equal halves. Flour your hands and flatten each half into a 12x8 rectangle. Fold the short side over to about half of the rectangle. Then fold the opposite side overlapping the first fold by about half an inch. Press flat again and starting from the short end roll the dough tightly into a loaf.

Set each loaf seam side down into a greased loaf pan. Cover the loaves with a towel. Let them rise for 45 minutes.

Bake the loaves in a preheated 390°F oven for about 40 minutes. With heat resistant gloves, remove the loaves from the oven and let them cool on a wire rack.

Raisin Bread

Ingredients:

- 1 tablespoon dry yeast.
- 2 cups warm (110°F) milk.
- 2 tablespoons soft butter
- 2 tablespoons sugar
- 1 cup raisins
- ½ teaspoon cinnamon
- Pinch nutmeg
- Approximately 6 cups unbleached all-purpose flour.
- 1 teaspoon salt.

Yield: 2 medium-size loaves.

In a 6 quart mixing bowl dissolve the yeast in the milk. Add the remaining ingredients and work them into dough.

Turn the dough out onto a lightly floured surface and knead it for about 7 minutes, until the dough is smooth and somewhat elastic.

Return the dough to the mixing bowl and cover it with a clean towel. Let the dough rise in a warm place for about 1 hour.

Divide the dough into 2 equal halves. Flour your hands and flatten each half into a 12x8 rectangle. Fold the short side over to about half of the rectangle. Then fold the opposite side overlapping the first fold by about half an inch. Press flat again and starting from the short end roll the dough tightly into a loaf.

Set each loaf seam side down into a greased loaf pan. Cover the loaves with a towel. Let them rise for about 45 minutes.

Bake the loaves in a preheated 390°F oven for about 40 minutes. With heat resistant gloves, remove the loaves from the oven and let them cool on a wire rack.

Buttermilk Bread

Ingredients:

- 1 tablespoon dry yeast.
- 2 cups warm (110°F) buttermilk.
- 2 tablespoons soft butter
- 2 tablespoons sugar
- Approximately 6 cups unbleached all-purpose flour.
- 1 teaspoon salt.

Yield: 2 medium-size loaves.

In a 6 quart mixing bowl dissolve the yeast in the buttermilk. Add the remaining ingredients and work them into dough.

Turn the dough out onto a lightly floured surface and knead it for about 7 minutes, until the dough is smooth and somewhat elastic.

Return the dough to the mixing bowl and cover it with a clean towel. Let the dough rise in a warm place for about 1 hour.

Divide the dough into 2 equal halves. Flour your hands and flatten each half into a 12x8 rectangle. Fold the short side over to about half of the rectangle. Then fold the opposite side overlapping the first fold by about half an inch. Press flat again and starting from the short end roll the dough tightly into a loaf.

Set each loaf seam side down into a greased loaf pan. Cover the loaves with a towel. Let them rise for 45 minutes.

Bake the loaves in a preheated 390°F oven for about 40 minutes. With heat resistant gloves, remove the loaves from the oven and let them cool on a wire rack.

Introduction to Whole Grain Breads

In the olden times whole grain breads were a major part of the people's diet. This played an important part on their health and longevity. Usually, bread was not just an accompaniment. Most of the time, it was the major part of their meals.

When I was growing up in the Flanders, our evening meals in the winter time consisted of heavy grainy bread with soups, and/or with some meat and lots of roasted vegetables. In the summer we enjoyed our hardy bread with cheese or cold cuts and salads. A lot of the times we just had slices of bread with butter and a dark brown homemade beer called "bock" beer. The focus of our meals was on the quality of the crusty and flavorful loaf.

In a good quality loaf you can taste the grain it is made from. Such bread is very satisfying and it quenches hunger quickly. Also, being slower to digest, it will not contribute to a weight problem. Sure, it is easier and more convenient to purchase commercial bread. However, there is nothing that says "Welcome" or "Thank-you" better than the smell of freshly homemade bread. It will be a little more convenient and easier to bake enough loaves for a week or two and then freeze the ones that are not consumed in one day. To freeze the bread, let it cool completely and then wrap it airtight in a plastic bag. Place it in the freezer. To defrost when you need a loaf, take it out the freezer and leave it wrapped at room temperature for about two hours. After removing the wrapper, you can re-heat the loaf in an oven or in a microwave for a few minutes and it will taste just like freshly baked.

Again, as I mentioned before, make sure that all the ingredients that you use in making bread including the flour, are at room temperature. This is one of the secrets in good bread baking. Enjoy baking and then "iedere dag is een feestdag"—every day is a feast day!

Honey Bran Bread

Ingredients:

- 1½ tablespoons dry yeast
- 2 cups warm (110°F.) water
- ¼ cup honey
- 2 tablespoons butter
- 1 cup miller's wheat bran
- Approximately 5 cups unbleached all-purpose flour
- 1 teaspoon salt

Yield: 2 medium-size loaves.

In a 6-quart mixing bowl, dissolve the yeast in the water. Add all the remaining ingredients and work them into dough.

Turn the dough out onto a lightly floured surface and knead it for about 7 minutes or until the dough is smooth and somewhat elastic.

Return the dough to the mixing bowl and cover it with a towel. Let the dough rise in a warm place for about 1 hour.

Divide the dough into 2 equal halves. Flour your hands and flatten each half into a 12x8 rectangle. Fold the short side over half of the rectangle and then fold the other side over the first fold overlapping it about half an inch. Press it flat again and starting with the short side, roll the dough like a jelly roll, into a loaf. Repeat with the other half of the dough.

Set the loaves seam side down into greased loaf pans and let them rise again in a warm place for about 45 minutes.

Bake the loaves in a pre-heated 390°F. oven for about 40 minutes or until golden brown.
With heat resistant gloves, remove the pans from the oven. Remove the loaves from the pans and let the loaves cool on a wire rack.

Oat bread

Ingredients:

- 1 tablespoon dry yeast
- 2 cups warm (110°F.) milk
- 2 tablespoons soft butter
- 1 tablespoon sugar
- ¼ cup quick oats
- Approximately 5¼ cups unbleached all-purpose flour
- 1 teaspoon salt

Yield: 2 medium-size loaves.

In a 6-quart mixing bowl, dissolve the yeast in the milk. Add all the remaining ingredients and work them into dough.

Turn the dough out onto a lightly floured surface and knead it for about 7 minutes or until the dough is smooth and somewhat elastic.

Return the dough to the mixing bowl and cover it with a towel. Let the dough rise in a warm place for about 1 hour.

Divide the dough into 2 equal halves. Flour your hands and flatten each half into a 12x8 rectangle. Fold the short side over half of the rectangle and then fold the other side over the first fold overlapping it about half an inch. Press it flat again and starting with the short side, roll the dough like a jelly roll, into a loaf. Repeat with the other half of the dough.

Set the loaves seam side down into greased loaf pans and let them rise again in a warm place for about 45 minutes.

Bake the loaves in a pre-heated 390°F. oven for about 40 minutes or until golden brown.
With heat resistant gloves, remove the pans from the oven. Remove the loaves from the pans and let the loaves cool on a wire rack.

Rye Bread

Ingredients:

- 1½ tablespoons dry yeast
- 2 cups warm (110°F.) water
- 1 tablespoon brown sugar
- 1 tablespoon soft butter
- 1 cup rye flour
- Approximately 5 cups unbleached all-purpose flour
- 1 teaspoon salt

Yield: 2 medium-size loaves.

In a 6-quart mixing bowl, dissolve the yeast in the water. Add all the remaining ingredients and work them into dough.

Turn the dough out onto a lightly floured surface and knead it for about 7 minutes or until the dough is smooth and somewhat elastic.

Return the dough to the mixing bowl and cover it with a towel. Let the dough rise in a warm place for about 1 hour.

Divide the dough into 2 equal halves. Flour your hands and flatten one half of the dough into a 12x8 rectangle. Fold the short side over half of the rectangle and then fold the other side over the first fold overlapping it about half an inch. Press it flat again and starting with the short side, roll the dough like a jelly roll, into a loaf. Repeat with the other half of the dough.

Set the loaves seam side down into greased loaf pans and let them rise again in a warm place for about 45 minutes.

Bake the loaves in a pre-heated 390°F. oven for about 40 minutes or until golden brown.

With heat resistant gloves, remove the pans from the oven. Remove the loaves from the pans and let the loaves cool on a wire rack.

Three Grain Bread

Ingredients:

- 1 tablespoon dry yeast
- 2 cups warm (110°F.) water
- ½ cup rye flour
- ½ cup whole wheat flour
- ½ cup oats
- Approximately 4½ cups unbleached all-purpose flour
- 1 teaspoon salt

Yield: 2 medium-size loaves.

In a 6-quart mixing bowl, dissolve the yeast in the water. Add all the remaining ingredients and work them into dough.

Turn the dough out onto a lightly floured surface and knead it for about 7 minutes or until the dough is smooth and somewhat elastic.

Return the dough to the mixing bowl and cover it with a towel. Let the dough rise in a warm place for about 1 hour.

Divide the dough into 2 equal halves. Flour your hands and flatten each half into a 12x8 rectangle. Fold the short side over half of each rectangle and then fold the other side over the first fold overlapping it about half an inch. Press them flat again and starting with the short side, roll them like jelly rolls.

Set the loaves seam side down into loaf pans and let them rise again in a warm place for about 45 minutes.

Bake the loaves in a pre-heated 390°F. oven for about 40 minutes or until golden brown.

With heat resistant gloves, remove the pans from the oven. Remove the loaves from the pans and let the loaves cool on a wire rack.

Whole Wheat Bread

Ingredients:

- 1 tablespoon dry yeast
- 2 cups warm (110°F.) water
- 2 cups whole wheat flour
- Approximately 4 cups unbleached all-purpose flour
- 1 teaspoon salt

Yield: 2 medium-size loaves.

In a 6-quart mixing bowl, dissolve the yeast in the water. Add all the remaining ingredients and work them into dough.

Turn the dough out onto a lightly floured surface and knead it for about 7 minutes or until the dough is smooth and somewhat elastic.

Return the dough to the mixing bowl and cover it with a towel. Let the dough rise in a warm place for about 1 hour.

Divide the dough into 2 equal halves. Flour your hands and flatten each half into a 12x8 rectangle. Fold the short side over half of the rectangle and then fold the other side over the first fold overlapping it about half an inch. Press it flat again and starting with the short side, roll it like a jelly roll, to make a loaf. Repeat with the other half of the dough.

Set the loaves seam side down into greased loaf pans and let them rise again in a warm place for about 45 minutes.

Bake the loaves in a pre-heated 390°F. oven for about 40 minutes or until golden brown.

With heat resistant gloves, remove the pans from the oven. Remove the loaves from the pans and let the loaves cool on a wire rack.

Horse Bread

This delicious bread is very healthy. It is very high in fiber and low in sodium. It also is totally free of fat and sugar.

To begin with, mix 1 lb. of wheat bran with 2½ lbs. of whole rye flour. This recipe calls for 6 cups of this mixture. The rest of the mixture can be stored in the refrigerator for the next baking time.

Ingredients:

- 2 cups warm (110°F.) water
- ¾ teaspoon dry yeast
- 6 cups of the wheat and rye mixture as described above
- ¾ teaspoon salt

Yield: 2 medium size loaves

Place the water, the yeast and the flour into an electric mixer. Mix at low speed for about 5 minutes. Then add the salt and mix at low speed for about 15 minutes, scraping the bowl every 5 minutes.

Let the dough rise for about 1 hour.

Punch the dough down and divide it into 2 equal parts. Shape each part into an oblong loaf.

Set the loaves seam side down onto a greased baking sheet. Cover it with a towel and let the loaves rise for about 1 hour.

Bake the loaves in a pre-heated 400°F. oven for 30 minutes. Turn the oven heat down to 350°F, and bake for a full hour more, making the total baking time about 90 minutes.

With heat resistant gloves remove the loaves from the oven and the baking sheet and allow them to cool on a wire rack.

Mediterranean Pocket Bread, or Zakken Brood

Ingredients:

- 1 tablespoon dry yeast
- 2 cups warm (110°F.) water
- 1 cup whole wheat flour
- Approximately 5 cups unbleached all-purpose flour
- 1 teaspoon salt

Yield: 24 small-size pocket loaves.

In a 6-quart mixing bowl, dissolve the yeast in the water. Add all the remaining ingredients and work them into dough.

Turn the dough out onto a lightly floured surface and knead it for about 7 minutes or until the dough is smooth and somewhat elastic.

Return the dough to the mixing bowl and cover it with a towel. Let the dough rise in a warm place for about 20 minutes.

Divide the dough into 24 equal pieces. Flour your hands and shape each piece like a golf ball. Let these round pieces of dough rise in a warm place for about 10 minutes.

With a rolling pin, roll flat each round piece of dough to the size of a small saucer 5½ to 6 inches in diameter. Let these pieces rise again for 10 minutes.

There are two choices now to proceed:

1. The Mediterranean method for crispy pocket bread, or:
2. The Flemish method for soft and chewy pocket bread.

1—The Mediterranean Method:

Lightly grease 4 12x18 baking sheets. Place on each sheet 6 flat round pieces of dough. Let them rise on a warm place for about 10 minutes.

Pre-heat the oven at a high temperature of about 450°F. On the lowest rack of the oven, place two baking sheets with six flat round pieces of dough on each. Let them bake for 1½ minutes. Then, quickly move them to a higher rack and let them bake for about 5 minutes, or until all the pieces have puffed up nicely. With heat resistant gloves remove the baking sheets from the oven and let the pocket breads cool on a wire rack. They will deflate while cooling. Repeat the process with the flat round pieces of dough on the remaining baking sheets.

2—The Flemish Method:

Place 6 round flat pieces of dough on a very hot 11x19 griddle. When the pieces become blistery on top, turn them quickly over with a spatula. Grill the pieces until they puff up. With the spatula remove them from the griddle and let them cool on a wire rack. They will deflate as they cool. Repeat the process until all the pieces are done. This method works real well with an electric griddle with a non-stick surface.

Scheele's Secret Rye Spice Recipe

This rye spice recipe has been a trade secret in our family's bakery for generations. It makes for very flavorful rye breads.

- 1 tablespoon Caraway seeds
- 1 tablespoon Coriander seeds
- ½ teaspoon Anise seeds
- ½ teaspoon Fennel seeds
- ½ teaspoon Cumin seeds

Place all the seeds in a clean spice or coffee mill. Grind them well. To preserve the prime flavor store them in a clean tight lidded jar away from the light and any source of heat.

Scheele's Cheese Rye Bread

This very flavorful bread was one of the best sellers at our bakery in Axel, The Netherlands. After you have a taste of it, this loaf might become one of your favorites.

Ingredients:

- 1 tablespoon dry yeast
- 2 cups warm (110°F.) water
- 1½ cups shredded Gouda cheese
- 1½ cups rye flour
- 2 teaspoons rye spice * (see recipe above)
- Approximately 4½ cups unbleached all-purpose flour
- 1 teaspoon salt

Yield: 2 medium-size loaves.

In a 6-quart mixing bowl, dissolve the yeast in the water. Add all the remaining ingredients and work them into dough.

Turn the dough out onto a lightly floured surface and knead it for about 7 minutes or until the dough is smooth and somewhat elastic.

Return the dough to the mixing bowl and cover it with a towel. Let the dough rise in a warm place for about 1 hour.

Divide the dough into 2 equal halves. Flour your hands and flatten each half into a 12x8 rectangle. Fold the short side over half of the rectangle and then fold the other side over the first fold overlapping it about half an inch. Press it flat again and starting with the short side, roll it like a jelly roll, to make a loaf. Repeat with the other half of the dough. Set the loaves seam side down onto a greased baking sheet. Cover the loaves with a towel and let them rise again in a warm place for about 45 minutes.

Bake the loaves in a pre-heated 390°F. oven for about 45 to 50 minutes or until golden brown.

With heat resistant gloves, remove the baking sheets from the oven. Remove the loaves from the baking sheets and let the loaves cool on a wire rack.

Weekend Tunnel Bread

This bread originally started as a joke by one of the hired man at my grandfather's bakery. One Saturday morning there were 2 small batches of leftover dough; one for white bread and the other for brown bread. As a joke, the hired man used a rolling pin to roll the white dough into a 7x7 flat square. Then with his hands he rolled the brown dough into a 7 inches long rope-like strand. He then placed the brown rope of dough onto the square of white dough. He rolled the white dough all around the brown dough and made it into a loaf that looked like a tunnel from the narrow ends after it was baked.

Later that day he sold this loaf to a family with 4 children. When the mother asked him about the name of the bread, he told her that it was: "Weekend Tunnel Bread".

On early Monday morning the mother came back to the bakery and ordered 3 more loaves of that wonderful "Weekend Tunnel Bread". She said the children just loved that bread and it was instantly devoured. They loved white bread yet now had the benefit of the whole grain also. She thought it was the best idea we ever had in making bread. She also spread the word all around and soon we couldn't keep up with the demand. What started as a joke became a popular money maker. The worker that started it was well compensated and so we all had a good laugh all the way to the bank.

To make this bread you will need to use two different recipes. One could be for the soft white bread and the other for the honey bran bread. Start by first making the dough for the white bread. Then make the dough for the bran bread. Since the dough for the latter naturally rises a little faster it is best to make the white dough first. Let them both rise for 30 minutes.

Divide each lump of dough into 4 parts, for a total of 8 pieces, which will make 4 loaves of Tunnel Bread. With a rolling pin roll flat the 4 pieces of white dough into 7x7 squares. Then roll the 4 pieces of bran dough into 7 inches long ropes or strands. Place one bran rope of dough onto each square of white dough. Roll the white square all around the bran rope of dough to make it into a loaf, with the bran dough in the center.

Place each loaf into a lightly greased baking sheet. Let the loaves rise for about 40 minutes in a warm place.

Bake the loaves in a pre-heated 390°F. oven for about 45 minutes.

With heat resistant gloves remove the loaves from the oven and from the baking sheets and let the loaves cool off on a wire rack.

Note: The ingredients in the recipes can be cut in half in order to obtain 2 loaves.

Introduction to Old World Pumpernickel

A frequently asked question is: "What is the difference between European and American Pumpernickel?"

To start out with, Pumpernickel is a misnomer. It is a derivative of an East Frisian word "Kumphernickel' meaning "flatulence" or "full of gas". The word denotes a very coarse ground rye meal and it describes its effect on the human digestive system. However, genuine European pumpernickel is very friendly to the palate and to the digestion. It is very different to what Americans call pumpernickel.

European pumpernickel is very unique and it is the result of a very long and cool fermentation process. The slow fermentation method makes for a loaf that is not as airy, and it is denser than the American version. The real difference though, is in the flavor. It is very satisfying, rich and savory.

Most commercial pumpernickel that one sees in our local supermarkets is made with a mixture of pumpernickel flour, bleached white flour, and malted flour. The white flour is bleached to preserve and prolong its shelf life. The malted flour is added to eliminate the need for a long slow rising of the dough. However, what is gained in time is lost in flavor. Also, most loaves have added to them artificial colors and lots of fat, salt and sugar, besides many chemical ingredients.

Some bread cook book recipes call for the tinting of the pumpernickel dough. Some recommend the use of instant coffee, cocoa, etc. I have seen some that even recommend brown gravy mix powders and beef bouillon granules. Some of these recipes go by the name of "Black Russian Rye". This is very amusing not only to Russians, but also to all European bread bakers.

In Europe rye flour is often used in combination with wheat flour. In some areas on the Old Continent full whole grain rye is the main everyday staple. A particular strain of European rye grain is very dark. In Siberia this strain is called black wheat. This type of dark rye flour will make the loaf that is called Black Bread.

In ancient times all bread dough was raised slowly with wild yeast called a "sourdough starter". Now we have dry yeast and it is more convenient and easier to use it in bread making. Yet this comes at the cost of flavor and texture.

True pumpernickel has a wonderful crust that is chewy and savory. It should not be toasted, as toasting will cover over the special flavor of the slow raised rye bread. It makes for wonderful open faced sandwiches. It is delicious just with butter. Good pumpernickel bread is like good aged wine and good aged cheese. A shortcut in the process is a shortcut in taste.

Authentic European Pumpernickel should always be somewhat chewy, but never tough. It should not separate in your mouth as you bite into it. It should not be tender or flaky like a pastry. The texture is definitely a little dense or compact. The crust should be crackly and crisp. The crumb should be moist and soft yet at the same time slightly chewy. The crumb should never be silky. When you cut into the loaf the crumb should have a barely perceptible pleasant yeasty aroma. It has a deep earthy rye grain flavor. This deep intense undefinable flavor is unobtainable except by the cool slow and long rising procedure.

To allow the Pumpernickel dough to develop its delightful unique flavor through this slow, overnight method, the following steps are necessary:

> 1—After the first full and complete rise, punch the dough down and place it in a ceramic or glass bowl, or in a non-chemical plastic bag.

2—Store it in a refrigerator for 24 hours.

3—Take the dough out of the refrigerator and shape it into a loaf. Let the loaf slowly come to room temperature and fully rise again.

This long cool rising will increase the acetic acid content of the dough that will give the bread its unique delicious flavor.

Traditionally Pumpernickel bread should never be baked in a pan. It should be baked on a prepared baking sheet, or better yet, on a hot baking stone to imitate to an extent the exquisite effect of an adobe oven hearth.

With practice comes perfection. Yet even your first loaf baked using this slow fermentation process will give you a taste of what good Pumpernickel should be like and you will never go back to the store boughten kind that is loaded with sugar, fat and salt and laced with artificial colorings and flavorings. Contrary to popular belief, genuine European Pumpernickel is not fattening. The contents of the commercial version will add to a weight problem.

At a lecture I gave in Wyoming in 1988 about bread baking, someone asked me about the origin of the Pumpernickel bread. Since Biblical times people were fond of bread. The origin of Pumpernickel is obscure. In the Flemish tradition it had to do with the way they baked bread in the ancient villages. Usually there was a huge common oven that all the villagers used. The fornarius or oven master, would light the oven very early in the mornings, before day break.

Generally the oven would be hot and ready for baking around 5 or 6AM. This made it necessary for the women to rise before daybreak to start kneading the dough. This kneading had to be done by the light of an oil lamp or a candle. In the winter time many kitchens were cold as few people would keep a fire going thru the night. Some women learned that they could start making the dough in the late afternoon by the waning daylight hours and by using less yeast they could let the dough rise in a cold kitchen overnight and have it ready for baking before dawn the next morning. As an unexpected bonus they realized that their bread was a lot more flavorful than ordinarily. The discovery of the deeper flavor of Pumpernickel gave rise to a proverb: "Bake in haste and it will turn out in waste, especially the taste."

Scheele's Renown Pumpernickel Bread Spice

This spice recipe was a guarded secret at my grandfather's bakery for many generations. It makes indescribably delicious Pumpernickel bread. If you like to enjoy a very spicy loaf, just increase the amount of the spices. The next three recipes for Pumpernickel bread call for this spice blend. You might want to experiment making the bread without it, and then you will be astonished with the difference it makes in taste.

- 250 grams (8.75 oz.) Caraway seeds
- 200 grams (7 oz.) Coriander seeds
- 100 grams (3.50 oz.) Cardamom seeds. (Break the white greenish husks and discard them. Use the small dark seeds without the husks.)
- 50 grams (1.75 oz.) Anise seeds
- 50 grams (1.75 oz.) Fennel seeds
- 50 grams (1.75 oz.) Cumin seeds
- 30 grams (1 oz.) Ground Ginger

Mix all the different seeds along with the powdered ginger thoroughly before grinding them. Grind this mixture extra fine in a clean spice or coffee mill. Store the ground spices in a glass container and close the lid tightly. To ensure freshness and to preserve the prime flavor, store the container in a cool dry place away from the light.

The superlative Pumpernickel Loaf

This exquisite loaf will immerse you in a true gourmet experience of the Old Continent. It looks like it starts as a sourdough, yet the process is quite different. Normal sourdough is made without salt, and at room temperature. For this Pumpernickel the slow, cool, long rising method of about 48 hours, will fully develop a natural micro flora that normally dwells in the whole rye flour. This micro flora along with the onion juice and the vinegar will produce a special lactic acid that will determine the unique and delicious flavor of the finished loaf.

Ingredients:

- ½ cup cool (100°F.) water
- 1 teaspoon onion juice
- 1 teaspoon cider vinegar
- ¼ teaspoon dry yeast
- 1¼ cups whole rye flour
- ¼ teaspoon salt.

In a small (2 quart size) glass or ceramic bowl mix all the ingredients thoroughly. Cover the bowl with a plastic wrap and let the mixture ferment in a cool place for about 48 hours.

After 48 hours, in a 6-quart mixing bowl dissolve:

- 1 teaspoon dry yeast
- 1½ cups warm (110°F.) water

Add the fermented rye mixture from the 2-quart bowl. Mix it well. Now add:

- 1¼ cups dark rye flour
- 2 cups whole wheat flour
- 1¼ cups unbleached all-purpose flour
- 1½ tablespoons molasses
- 1½ tablespoons sorghum

- 1 teaspoon pumpernickel spice (recipe on page 56)
- 1 teaspoon salt.

Mix all the ingredients well and work them into dough that is soft and sticky. Turn the dough out onto a lightly floured surface and knead it for about 7 minutes until it is smooth and somewhat elastic. Return the dough to the mixing bowl and cover it with a towel.

Let the dough rise for about 1 hour. Then, divide the dough into 2 equal parts.

Flour your hands, and flatten each part of the dough into an 8x6 rectangle. Starting from the short end fold one side over to the middle and then fold the other side overlapping the first fold about ½ inch. Press flat again and starting from the short end tightly roll each rectangle like a jelly roll to form two oblong loaves.

Set the loaves seam side down onto a baking sheet that has been liberally dusted with corn meal. Cover the loaves with a towel and let them rise again for about 1 hour.

Bake the loaves in a pre-heated 390°F. oven for about 1 hour.

With heat resistant gloves remove the loaves from the baking sheets and let them cool on a wire rack.

Slow Rise Plain Pumpernickel

This is truly very healthy bread. It has no added sweeteners or shortening. Yet it has a delightful and very satisfying flavor. It is one of the favorites in the Flanders region of Europe.

Ingredients:

- 2 cups warm (110°F.) water
- 1 teaspoon dry yeast
- 3 cups whole wheat flour
- 3 cups whole rye flour
- 1 teaspoon pumpernickel spice (recipe on page 56)
- 1 teaspoon salt

Yield: 2 medium size loaves.

In a 6-quart mixing bowl dissolve the yeast in the warm water.

Add all the remaining ingredients. Mix them well and work them into dough. Turn the dough out onto a lightly floured surface and knead it for about 7 minutes until it is smooth and somewhat elastic. Return the dough to the mixing bowl and cover it with a towel.

Let the dough rise for about 1 hour.

Punch the dough down. Now place the dough into a glass or ceramic lidded container or in a plastic bag and store it in the refrigerator for about 24 hours.

After 24 hours remove the dough from the refrigerator, divide it into two parts and shape each part into a round or an oblong loaf.

Set the loaves onto a lightly greased baking sheet. Cover the loaves with a towel and let them slowly come to room temperature, letting them rise from about 2 or 3 hours, depending on the room temperature. This heavy dough will only increase to about 70% in bulk.

Bake the loaves in a pre-heated 390°F. oven for about 1 hour.

With heat resistant gloves remove the loaves from the baking sheets and let them cool on a wire rack.

Slow Rise Dark Aromatic Pumpernickel

This delectable bread is a winner in taste and aroma. It gets lots of raves when presented at the dinner table on an attractive basket with a decorative towel. It goes well with Gouda cheese and a nice glass of red wine.

Ingredients:

- 1 cup warm (110°F.) water
- 1 cup warm (110°F.) plain yogurt
- 1 teaspoon dry yeast
- 3 cups whole wheat flour
- 2¾ cups whole rye flour
- 2 tablespoons soft butter
- 2 tablespoons molasses
- 1 teaspoon pumpernickel spice (recipe on page 56)
- 1 teaspoon salt

Yield: 2 medium size loaves.

In a 6-quart mixing bowl dissolve the yeast in the warm water.

Add all the remaining ingredients. Mix them well and work them into dough. Turn the dough out onto a lightly floured surface and knead it for about 7 minutes until it is smooth and somewhat elastic. Return the dough to the mixing bowl and cover it with a towel.

Let the dough rise for about 1 hour.

Punch the dough down. Now place the dough into a glass or ceramic lidded container or in a plastic bag and store it in the refrigerator for about 24 hours.

After 24 hours remove the dough from the refrigerator, divide it into two parts and shape each part into a round or an oblong loaf.

Set the loaves onto a lightly greased baking sheet. Cover the loaves with a towel and let them slowly come to room temperature, letting them rise from about 2 or 3 hours, depending on the room temperature. This heavy dough will only increase to about 70% in bulk.

Bake the loaves in a pre-heated 390°F. oven for about 1 hour.

With heat resistant gloves remove the loaves from the baking sheets and let them cool on a wire rack.

Russian Wheat and Yeast Free Sour Pumpernickel

This bread is not only delicious and nutritious; it is a bonus for people that are allergic to either wheat or yeast, or both.

Starter ingredients:

- ½ cup dark rye flour
- ½ cup lukewarm (110°F.) water

In a glass or ceramic bowl mix the starter ingredients well. Cover the bowl tightly with plastic wrap to keep wild yeast cells out. Let this mixture ferment in a warm (75°F) place for about 4 days (100 hours).

Then, add and stir in the starter mixture:

- ½ cup dark rye flour
- ½ cup lukewarm (110°F) water

Cover the bowl again and placed it in a warm place for 24 hours. This mixture will bubble and have a yeasty-like aroma. All of this starter will be needed to make this Russian bread.

Ingredients for the dough:

- 4½ cups dark rye flour
- 1 cup warm (110°F.) water
- 1 teaspoon salt.

In a 6-quart mixing bowl mix well the ingredients for the dough. Add all of the starter ingredients. This will make very sticky, wet dough. Mix it thoroughly for about 7 minutes.

Let the dough rise in the bowl for about 3 hours.

This wet dough will be difficult to shape. Wet your hands with cold water and scoop the dough into two well-greased pans. Cover the pans with plastic wrap and let the dough rise until it is close to the top of the pans. Depending on the room temperature and other conditions, like the strength of the starter, this may take from 2 to 6 hours.

Remove the plastic wrap and bake the loaves in a pre-heated 420°F. oven for about 1 hour.

With heat resistant gloves remove the loaves from the oven and let them cool on a wire rack.

Village Pumpernickel

This very flavorful bread comes from a very Old Dutch recipe. It is unique and distinct from other pumpernickels and a favorite of the Flemish village where my grandfather had his bakery. For centuries the village women would prepare the dough at home in the evenings, letting it rise overnight. Then, in the early hours of the next morning they would bring the loaves to the communal oven for baking.

Ingredients:

- 2 cups warm (110°F.) potato cooking water
- ½ teaspoon dry yeast
- 3 cups whole wheat flour
- 3 cups whole rye flour
- 2oz. soft butter
- 2 tablespoons molasses
- 1 teaspoon salt

Yield: 1 large loaf.

In a 6-quart mixing bowl dissolve the yeast in the warm potato cooking water.

Add all the remaining ingredients. Mix them well and work them into dough. Turn the dough out onto a lightly floured surface and knead it for about 7 minutes until it is smooth and somewhat elastic. Return the dough to the mixing bowl and cover it with a towel.

Let the dough rise for about 2½ hours.

Punch the dough down. Now place the dough into a glass or ceramic lidded container or in a plastic bag and store it in the refrigerator overnight.

The next morning, remove the dough from the refrigerator, and shape it into a round or an oblong loaf.

Set the loaf onto a lightly greased baking sheet. Cover the loaf with a towel and let it rise again. This loaf will rise very slowly because it has only half of the normal yeast. It may take from 6 to 8 hours to double in bulk, depending on the room temperature.

Bake the loaves in a pre-heated 390°F. oven for about 1 hour.

With heat resistant gloves remove the loaves from the baking sheets and let them cool on a wire rack. If you prefer a softer crust, brush the loaf lightly with butter.

Light and Sweet Betrothal Pumpernickel

When Janeke, the town matchmaker made a match she would order this bread from our bakery. This is very light and sweet pumpernickel laced with black currants. It was made especially for engagements and consisted of two loaves baked together in one pan. The matchmaker would tie two tulips to the bread. Presenting it to the girl's father, the matchmaker would kiss one of the tulips. If the father accepted the match, he would kiss the other tulip. Then, he would place the twin loaves on the table, slice it and serve the first slice to the matchmaker. If the match was refused, the father would simply return the bread without kissing the tulip.

Ingredients:

- 2 cups warm (110°F.) water
- 1 teaspoon dry yeast
- 4 cups unbleached all-purpose flour
- 2 cups whole rye flour
- 1 cup black currants
- ½ cup light molasses
- ¼ stick melted butter
- 1 teaspoon salt

Yield: 3 twin sets of small size loaves baked together in 3 pans.

In a 6-quart mixing bowl dissolve the yeast in the warm water.

Add all the remaining ingredients. Mix them well and work them into dough. Turn the dough out onto a lightly floured surface and knead it for about 7 minutes until it is smooth and somewhat elastic. Return the dough to the mixing bowl and cover it with a towel.

Let the dough rise for about 1 hour, in a warm place.

Divide the dough into six equal parts. Shape each part into a long thin loaf.

Place two loaves side by side into a buttered bread pan. Repeat the same with the next two loaves, until you have three sets of twins in three pans. Cover the loaves with towels and let them rise in a warm place for about 40 minutes.

Bake the loaves in a pre-heated 375°F. oven for about 1 hour.

With heat resistant gloves remove the loaves from the baking sheets and let them cool on a wire rack.

Romance and bread—what better combination?

For the wedding day, the couple would be presented with a special Bundt loaf as a courtesy of our bakery. In German this loaf was called "Kugelhopf". In the Flanders we called it "Tulband".

For the recipe of a Wedding Tulband, please see my book "Old World Bread", pages 128-130.

The History of Spelt Bread

In our modern times spelt bread is enjoying a revival. Not only it is sought after by the people who have allergies to wheat or celiac disease, but it has also become a treat to connoisseurs all over the world.

Spelt bread has a delicious nutty flavor which is very pleasing to the palate. It is very satisfying and very nutritious. It has many health benefits.

This grain has been cultivated since the beginning of times. Well over 3,500 years ago, Moses wrote about the spelt harvest of Egypt, at Exodus chapter 9 verse 32. It was popular in the early Greek culture. The Roman scholar Gaius Plinius (23-79AD) wrote that the spelt bread was the everyday staff and mainstay of the Roman troops that marched across the European Continent. It was widely cultivated in Asia Minor and during the Middle Ages spelt was very common in Southern Europe and in the Middle East.

Some have wrongly called spelt an inferior kind of wheat. However, it is only inferior in a commercial sense. Modern wheat has been bred by bioengineers to produce extra strong gluten. It was also engineered to contain almost twice the amount of gluten it originally had, and in addition, for the plants to produce bigger quantities of grain per acreage and to be resistant to pests. Wheat is also specially bred for easier processing and milling. Spelt on the other hand, has gone thru none of these changes. It is the same grain that was cultivated in olden times.

The bread dough from modern wheat rises higher and it makes for a much lighter loaf. Because the gluten is much tougher, it has a high tolerance for mechanical kneading and processing. However tougher gluten is very hard to digest for some people. Also, the addition of hydrogenated oil, extra amounts of sugar and salt and the various chemical additives used to prolong shelf life are not a health bonus.

From the viewpoint of health, nutrition and flavor spelt bread is much superior to modern wheat. Spelt is much higher in complex B-vitamins, iron and potassium. Also, the proteins (the gluten) are very different than wheat. They are more fragile and much easier to digest. Spelt berries are naturally darker in color and higher in fiber. The flour will make for heavier, darker and grainier bread than wheat, yet a lot easier to the digestive system. The nutty flavor is very palatable and it gives a delectable sense of satisfaction.

Spelt flour can be substituted for wheat flour in almost every recipe. All one needs to do is to use a little less liquid. Spelt will absorb about 20% less liquid than the wheat flour. Since the proteins in the spelt flour are more fragile, there is a need to reduce the kneading and rising time of the dough. Over kneading and over rising is likely to collapse the loaf and it will produce extra compact and dense bread, more like a door stop. For best overall results, kneading time should be around 4 minutes, and the rising periods down to 30 minutes or slightly less. Also, the amount of yeast should be about 10% less than what is used in the regular wheat recipes.

Due to the fragility of the gluten and the lesser time used for kneading and rising, spelt bread is not a good choice to be made in bread machines. Bread machines will produce more and larger air pockets in the bread, and the texture will turn out grainier and dryer. Also there will be a lessening of flavor and quality. Spelt bread is best when done the conventional way.

After baking, cool the bread on a wire rack. Since spelt bread will keep fresh naturally longer than wheat, it is best to store it in a bread box, at room temperature. Do not wrap bread in plastic and store it in the refrigerator. You will know the difference yourself if when baking two loaves, store one in the refrigerator and the other at room temperature. Bread will keep well in the freezer, after placed in a plastic bag. It is best to slice it first, so that you can use only the amount of slices you need at a time, keeping the rest frozen. To defrost, leave the bread in the plastic bag and let it thaw out overnight at room temperature. Or, if you need it right away, remove the plastic bag and place the loaf into a pre-heated 325°F oven for about 10 to 15 minutes. Spelt bread should always be baked thoroughly. Since oven temperatures differ, after baking your loaves for 1 hour or until they are golden brown, remove a loaf with a heat resistant glove in one hand and with the other ungloved hand tap its bottom. If it sounds hollow, the bread is done. If not, replace it in the oven and bake it 10 minutes longer.

I know you will love spelt bread if you try it. "Love at first loaf" and you will become a happy spelt bread eater forever.

The Flemish Sponge Method for Spelt Bread

This sponge method will make for the best tasting spelt bread you ever had.

In this technique all the yeast called for in the recipe is dissolved in all the liquid prescribed, yet with only half of the flour mixed in. This will make for a soft batter or sponge.

Let the batter or sponge ferment for about 20 minutes.

Then, add the rest of the flour and the salt, and knead into dough for about 3½ minutes. Be careful not to over knead spelt dough.

Let the dough rise for about 30 minutes. It is best to let it rise a little less than more.

This is a simple process that originally started in the Flanders region of Europe and it is generally referred to as the Flemish Method. It creates spelt bread that is superior in texture and in flavor.

Regular Spelt Bread Made with Yeast

This tasty bread made with organic whole spelt flour is not only healthy but also delicious and it will keep fresh for days. It is a wonderful treat with sharp Cheddar cheese.

For best success, please measure all items accurately. Please, remember not to over knead or let the dough over rise.

Ingredients:

- ¾ teaspoon dry yeast
- 1¾ cups warm (110°F.) water
- 1 tablespoon dry milk
- 1 tablespoon canola oil
- Approximately 6 cups organic whole spelt flour
- 1 teaspoon salt

Yield: 2 medium size loaves

In a 6-quart mixing bowl dissolve the yeast in the warm water.

Mix the salt with the flour. Add them into the bowl with all the rest of the ingredients and work them into dough.

Turn the dough onto a lightly floured surface and knead it for about 4 minutes.

Return the dough to the mixing bowl and cover it with a towel. Let the dough rise for about 30 minutes.

Divide the dough into 2 equal parts and shape each part into an oblong loaf.

Set the loaves onto a baking sheet that has been lightly greased with vegetable shortening. Cover the loaves with a towel and let them rise again for 30 minutes.

Bake the loaves in a pre-heated 400° oven for 45 minutes or until golden brown.

With heat resistant gloves remove the loaves from the baking sheet and let them cool on a wire rack.

Wheat free and commercial yeast free spelt starter

Sourdough starter is a leaven that is living in a batter of flour and water. Before the industrial revolution almost all breads were made with a sour dough starter.

There are innumerable different strains of starters. Some are made with the wheat flour; others are made with commercial baker's yeast. Most commercial yeast is made from a single hyperactive genetically modified strain of a domesticated cousin of the elusive wild yeast. The wild yeast normally dwells on the outside of fruit and in the air all around us. Both wheat and commercial baker's yeast are common food allergens and should be avoided by people that are sensitive to them. However many who have such allergies seem to tolerate the natural wild yeast that dwells on the spelt kernels.

The micro flora that coats the outside of the spelt kernels has already adapted to their hosts and will work in a batter to make a vigorous starter. This strain is self-sustaining and it gets more vigorous with age. All what it needs is some spelt flour, water and a cozy warm temperature to start multiplying. It will feed on the natural sugars that are present in the whole spelt flour. As they multiply they give off carbon dioxide with its fermentation that will make the dough rise and will give the bread a much better flavor.

Since the wild yeast cells dwell naturally and abundantly only on the outside or the bran of the spelt kernel it is best to use only organic whole spelt flour, with all the bran included. I am not implying that the white spelt flour is sterile, only that the micro flora count in white spelt flour is too low to make a vigorous starter. Our aim is to capture as many wild yeast cells as possible and to encourage them to grow and multiply.

To start the process it is best to use a non-metal bowl that is thoroughly clean and scalded with boiling water, to make sure that no non desirable bacteria interferes in the starter. Do not use chlorinated water or salt in the starter. These will repress the micro flora that you are trying to encourage to grow. As soon as you placed the starter mixture in the bowl, cover it tightly with plastic wrap to keep any airborne wild yeast out. Place the bowl with its covered mixture in a cozy warm place away from any drafts. If at any point the starter develops a pinkish or greenish color or a strange odor, discard it. Some unwanted bacteria got a hold of it. A good starter has a light cream color and a clean yeasty aroma.

All starters develop at a slightly different rate of speed, depending on the season of the year, the atmospheric conditions and the room temperature. They will develop more quickly on hot humid summer days and slower on dry cold winters. Generally starters improve with age just like wine or aged cheese, and will develop a deeper flavor over time.

A note from this Flemish baker: With experimentation over the years I learned that when the starter is ready to be used you will get a much better and fuller flavor if you store it in the refrigerator to let it go dormant for about 4 days (100 hours). Then place it in a cozy (80-88°F.) place for about 8 to 10 hours, to warm it up. A nice and cozy place for it would be the inside of a gas oven with only the pilot light on or in an electric oven with the indoor oven light on. A cold starter will never work. So always make sure that starter comes to a warm room temperature before you use it.

A note of caution: Be wary of the mail order dehydrated sourdough cultures. Not all are free from wheat or commercial yeast. Even sometimes when they are advertised as free from wheat they may contain small amounts of it. This still could present a problem if you are allergic to wheat.

Commercial Yeast Free and Wheat Free Spelt Sourdough Starter

In a clean and sterile ceramic or glass bowl mix together:

- ½ cup organic whole spelt flour
- ½ cup tepid non-chlorinated water

Mix the ingredients well and cover the bowl tightly with plastic wrap.

Keep this mixture in a warm (80°F.) place, away from drafts for about 100 hours. Stir the mixture daily and cover it afterwards. After 100 hours this mixture will start to bubble. At this stage add and stir in:

- ½ cup organic whole spelt flour
- ½ cup tepid non chlorinated water
- Mix well again and cover it tightly with the plastic wrap so as to keep airborne wild yeast out. Let this mixture ferment in a warm (80°F.) place for about 50 hours, stirring it daily.

Then, add:

- 2 cups organic whole spelt flour
- 2 cups tepid non chlorinated water

Mix well and cover it tightly again. Let the mixture ferment again for 50 hours in the same warm place. Stir the starter daily.

The starter now should be bubbly and have a fruity yeasty aroma. Store the starter tightly wrapped in the refrigerator undisturbed (no stirring). About 8 to 10 hours before making the bread remove the starter from the refrigerator and let it warm up to reach a warm room temperature. A cold starter will not work.

Stir the starter thoroughly before pouring out the amount you need for making the bread. Keep the remaining starter covered tightly in the refrigerator for the next baking day. You will need to feed the starter every week with equal portions of spelt flour and water.

Sourdough 100% Whole Spelt Bread—Commercial Yeast and Wheat Free

This delicious and nutritious bread is very slow in rising. It makes for a very flavorful but compact loaf. This recipe has an ancient history and it has delighted generations of people. It will delight you also. It is worth the waiting time and the work involved.

Ingredients:

- 3 cups of spelt starter at room temperature (see recipe on page 77)
- Approximately 6 cups organic whole spelt flour
- 1 teaspoon salt

In a 6-quart mixing bowl mix all the ingredients and work them into dough.

Turn the dough out into a lightly floured surface and knead it for only 3 minutes. Do not over knead.

Return the dough to the mixing bowl and cover it tightly with plastic wrap. Let the dough rise in a warm (80°F.) place for about 8 to 9 hours.

Shape the dough into a loaf and set it seam side down into a lightly greased bread pan. Cover it with the plastic wrap and let it rise again in a warm place for about 10 hours.

Bake the loaf in a pre-heated 390°F. oven for 55 minutes to 1 hour or until golden brown.

With heat resistant gloves remove the bread from the oven and let it cool on a wire rack.

The blessing of our daily bread

Blessings upon the land
Coming from His hand
Rain upon the sowing
Sun upon the mowing
Wind to drive the flour mill
Wood to heat the oven grill
Sourdough, the primitive yeast
Salt that makes the bread a feast
All these blessings make us able
To bring daily bread to our table
May we never ever forget
The provider of our bread
If of blessings He would us deprive
That would ruin our staff of life
Without this staff for our support
Life expectancy is cut very short
No matter how you boast or moan
Man cannot live by bread alone
It all depends on how He will bless
Not on any ability we possess
Having plenty of bread on hand
Depends on the blessings upon the land
The greatest teacher wisely said
Thank Him for your daily bread.

The Dreamer

Late in the night
While sleeping in bed
I dream so bright
About baking bread
Mixing salt flour and yeast
Then pummeling the beast
Next I let the dough rest
Then I press a finger to test
To see if the dough did rise
Oh, my what a surprise
The yeast performed its feat
Time to bake in the oven's heat
Oh the fragrance while it cools
Impatiently I wait while I drool
Smear it thick with country butter
I surely will not mutter
Hunger I now redeem
All because of a dream

Who am I?

A short rhyming riddle, by C. Scheele

Daily we sustain the millions
Daily we die by the zillions
History would not be the same
If we had stayed out the game
We've been blamed for war and strife
We've been the prayers of your life
The Mayflower had us on board
Actually we were the precious hoard
In America we were unkenned
We are of European descent
Quickly we became popular
That's why we are now globular
Now we are in every land
We are always on hand
When you closely investigate
Our identity you can excavate.

Who am I, coronel? A wheat kernel

About the Author:

Charel Scheele, a descendent of several generations of European professional bread bakers who owned their business and a flour windmill, is a retired professional baker from the Dutch part of the Flanders.

He grew up in the family bread baking business, and he learned from a practical standpoint every aspect of the trade. He also graduated with high honors from two different European schools for professional bread bakers.

Charel has won many awards and blue ribbons for his Old World breads. He has authored several cookbooks on bread baking.

He has written this book of his life as a baker to relate exciting experiences and historical notes of events occurred before, during and after the Second World War, so that the history of life then will not be forgotten.

Charel found comfort in his studies of the Bible that helped him deal with the frustrations he experienced during the horrific times of the War. Bread making served as outlet for him to physically work out the emotions he endured at that time.

In this book he is sharing with the readers not only the history of his life but also his expertise in bread making. Since life now is not free of problems, to the delight of the readers he has also included authentic European bread recipes. The kneading and the punching of the dough are a soothing help to deal with negative emotions, and may result in a delightful loaf of bread that will bring joy and satisfaction.

The author, now in the eighth decade of his life, resides in New Mexico, where he still bakes bread for his own enjoyment.

Index

Printed in the United States
By Bookmasters